*Parish, the Thought*

# Parish, the Thought

A Memoir in Ministry

David B. Bowman

RESOURCE *Publications* • Eugene, Oregon

PARISH, THE THOUGHT
A Memoir in Ministry

Copyright © 2018 David B. Bowman. All rights reserved. Except for brief quotations in critical publications or reviews, no part of this book may be reproduced in any manner without prior written permission from the publisher. Write: Permissions, Wipf and Stock Publishers, 199 W. 8th Ave., Suite 3, Eugene, OR 97401.

Resource Publications
An Imprint of Wipf and Stock Publishers
199 W. 8th Ave., Suite 3
Eugene, OR 97401

www.wipfandstock.com

PAPERBACK ISBN: 978-1-5326-4424-5
HARDCOVER ISBN: 978-1-5326-4425-2
EBOOK ISBN: 978-1-5326-4426-9

Manufactured in the U.S.A.

Scripture quotations are from the *New Revised Standard Version*. Oxford: Oxford University Press, 1994.

For Dianne,

without whom . . .

# Contents

*Preface* | ix
*List of Abbreviations* | xi

Straight Talk from the Pulpit | 1
Engagement Beyond the Sanctuary | 25
Mission to the World | 41
That They May All Be One | 61
Conflict and Resolution | 77
On the Lighter Side | 101
Close to Home | 115
The Parish Church Building | 127
The People of the Parish | 139

*Bibliography* | 157

# Preface

I wish that long ago I had adopted the habit of keeping a journal. Alas, I failed to keep such a record. Consequently, what follows relies heavily on memory.

One knows how faulty, and sometimes even misleading, one's memory can be. Suppose a married couple goes through the same experience side by side. Years later one may remember the incident in detail and the spouse draw a complete blank. Or one may recall a conversation in which a certain remark is retained in memory, only later to hear a recording of the conversation and discover memory misconstrued the utterance.

While I have not kept a journal, I have kept rather complete files of Sunday bulletins, newsletters, and other parish related documents. Review of these papers has jostled my mind into remembrance or, in several cases, corrected, narrowed, or broadened what I remember. In one case, during a four-week venture in the two German states in 1985, I did keep a rather complete record of incidents and my observations.

A word about the title: "Parish, the Thought." Of course, the spelling is important. We would not want these memories to "perish" else why bother to record them. But "parish"—that's a whole different ball of wax. In its original usage, a parish is a designated geographical area making up an administrative district in a diocese. In the State of Louisiana divisions in the state, counties elsewhere, are named parishes. In more common USA parlance a pastor may refer to his or her congregational ministry area as "my parish." This area may extend twenty minutes travel time in any direction in a jagged, jigsaw pattern. Hence, thoughts about the parish.

These memories might well gather in chronological order. That plan failed to appeal to me. A similar pattern might identify in consecutive order the parish churches where I served and collect each memory around that time and space. That, while interesting, proved not compelling.

# Preface

So instead I offer vignettes that fall into the various categories of ministry. While I prefer this approach, it's not foolproof. For example, a pulpit word about amnesty for those who went abroad during the Vietnam era might well fall under "Social Action," rather than my choice of "Straight Talk from the Pulpit." Most memories, however, fit neatly into one category or another. Ministry is a kaleidoscope film. Only a few of those visions made it to this screen.

With an earned PhD I might well have found my way into some classroom to teach. Certainly adult education became my preferred form of parish ministry. But I understand myself well enough to know that I could have escaped into the world of ideas. The people of the parish—their faces, their needs, sorrows, joys, and hopes, helped keep me more grounded and more other centered. I suspect that's been a blessing, sometimes obvious, other times in disguise.

I regard this as an exercise in practical theology. The parish minister regularly carries out the theological task in preaching, mentoring, nurturing, and reaching out. The document reveals my concern both for personal and social faith, for private and public enactment of the faith once delivered to the saints.

Those who know me personally, as well as those who know me not at all, may find my theological/political/ethical stance hard to pigeon-hole. Some views may seem too leftist and others too rightist, too heretical, or too orthodox. Someone may ask, "How do they exist side-by-side in the same person?" At the very least, they will be seen as forthright. I claim them to be well considered. Whether they come across as persuasive, only the reader will know.

Perhaps this account will enable an ordained reader to draw parallels. Maybe the lay reader will gain insight into the life and work of the clergy and ideas about the ministry of all God's people. And could it be that someone standing at a distance from church life, through these memories, might be led to lend heart and hand? All or any of the above would make this labor worthwhile.

These parish scenes opened in New York, Michigan, Washington State, Iowa, Indiana, and California, leading a friend, Duane, to speak of me as "a wanderer in the earth." Hardly a unique situation for someone seeking to be a pilgrim on the way with Jesus, the Christ.

# List of Abbreviations

| | |
|---|---|
| AMA | American Missionary Association |
| Bethel | Bethel United Church of Christ |
| CCUCC | Community Congregational Church, United Church of Christ |
| CO | Conscientious Objector |
| CWS | Church World Service |
| EI | Ecumenical Institute |
| EKU | Evangelical Church of the Union (*Evangelische Kirche der Union*) |
| FOR | Fellowship of Reconciliation |
| FRG | Federal Republic of Germany (*Deutsche Bundesrepublik*) |
| GDR | German Democratic Republic (*Deutsche Demokratische Republik*) |
| HFH | Habitat for Humanity |
| NTU | Northwest Theological Union |
| Park | First (Park) Congregational Church |
| PPR | Pastor–Parish Relations |
| RLDS | Reorganized Church of Latter Day Saints |
| STU | School of Theology and Ministry |
| UCC | United Church of Christ |
| UCCC | United Church of Christ–Congregational |
| UCUP | United Church in University Place |
| UM | United Ministries |
| WAC | Washington Association of Churches |
| WSU | Washington State University |

# Straight Talk from the Pulpit

> It is possible to think of the Gospel and our preaching of it as . . . above all, and at no matter what risk, speaking the truth about the way things are.
>
> Frederick Buechner, *Telling the Truth: The Gospel as Tragedy, Comedy and Fairy Tale*[1]

---

1. Buechner, *Telling the Truth*, 7.

## What Shall I Preach?

MY EXPERIENCE AS A young person in the pew, listening to the sermon of the day, yielded no sense of pattern for expectation. After all, the pastor or evangelist would offer "what God had laid on his heart" in his private devotions. In other words, I grew up used to topical sermons, only related to the church year at Christmas, Easter, and Pentecost.

It puzzles me that I never questioned this pattern until well into my career. The homiletics class at Nazarene Theological Seminary offered no enlightenment on the yearly pattern from the pulpit. I only remember offering "practice sermons" to the class. I doubt I would have gone around the corner to hear Professor James McGraw preach anyway.

In my Associate capacity at First (Park) Congregational Church (Park), Grand Rapids, Michigan, where I spoke from the pulpit only occasionally, I continued to speak out what was on my mind. This means finding a topic or theme, then going to scripture to proof text one's point. The Congregational tradition, loose in its observance of the Christian year, offered me no encouragement to change.

When I arrived at my first singular pastorate at Community Congregational Church, United Church of Christ (CCUCC), in Pullman, Washington, in 1971, nothing changed. In fact, the pattern intensified. I determined to preach on Sunday what rose to my attention in the course of a week of pastoral duties. In retrospect, my effort reflected the "what God laid on my heart" pattern in a more secular vein. Sometimes this worked when my mind and heart were flooded with ideas. At other times I came to Friday, and sometimes even on Saturday, with a certain panic. "Opening my mouth to let the Spirit fill it," appealed to me not at all.

Speaking of spontaneous pulpit patterns, I followed in a parish a man who bragged that on Sunday mornings he walked over to the church, from the next-door parsonage, in those moments pursuing his only preparation of the day. As often as not he would refer to the week's sports events, speak personally of someone in the congregation (usually in a jocular vein), and draw out some spiritual or moral insight. Some folk liked it. Others were skeptical. Count me among the latter.

Only when I came to my second singular parish ministry in Tacoma, Washington, United Church in University Place (UCUP), did the light begin to dawn. While attending continuing education events at the Vancouver School of Theology, the virtues of lectionary preaching, concurrent with the church year, hovered into view. With determination, I began weekly study of the lectionary texts in order to find grist for the Sunday message. I experienced this new orientation as a sort of personal grace. Indeed, as the years incorporating this pattern moved along, I found my personal life revolving around the Christian year much more than around the secular calendar. That remains true to this day.

As with any virtue there exist deficits. The passing scene at times calls for attention from the pulpit. If a tornado roars through town, one may not stand behind the sacred desk and expound on the beatitudes, if that gospel lesson is assigned for the week.

I recall that once, following the impeachment of President Clinton, I spoke on the non-assigned gospel text, "So have no fear of them; for nothing is covered up that will not be uncovered, and nothing secret that will not become known" (Matt 10:26). Also, speaking to certain social issues prove somewhat difficult if the scriptures scarcely raise the subject, e.g., the societal scourge of gambling.

Another detriment to lectionary preaching occurs. Sometimes on a Monday one comes to the readings for the week and discovers no movement of mind or heart. That presents a challenge to be met and overcome. If hard work and prayerful diligence take place, perhaps someone will say after the service, "That word meant a lot to me. One of your best messages."

One must not leave the subject of pulpit patterns without dealing with the issue of relevance. It is true that occasions have risen when concerns, spiritual or social, occupy mind and heart while the assigned readings seem far afield. At that point one remembers the nature of Protestant preaching, namely, that the word comes from the sacred text, not one's own private preoccupations. One hopes that the faith, hope, and love presented in the text, and "poured through human personality" from the pulpit, will bear all the relevancy any faithful listener might need. Leave it to some other occasion for the man or woman of the cloth to share fondest ideas or personal hobby horses.

## Publish Glad Tidings

A central feature of communication in the parish continues to be the newsletter. Announcements of parish events, presentation of the parish calendar, listing of parish staff, reports of births, baptisms, weddings, and deaths consume much of the content. Often these days the newsletter arrives on-line.

The parish newsletters adopt a tradition of titles—"The Chimes," "Good News," "Voice of Faith," "The Messenger," etc. In large churches these appear weekly. In smaller churches once a month publication appears to be the rule.

One other feature, not mentioned above, is the article written by the minister, or in larger parishes, by rotating ministers. The content of these articles, read over time, reveal much about the author. For the most part these pieces render Dullsville exciting. Often one detects the minister sensed the publication deadline rushing down. Something must be said. Occasionally one finds someone who writes well about significant matters. I remember with pleasure a regular monthly piece from Rev. Richard Coombs, Dean of the Episcopal Cathedral of St. John the Evangelist, in Spokane, Washington.

Too often one encounters those clergy who use the newsletter space to talk about themselves *ad nauseum*. They speak of their trials, their joy in the ministry, their renewed spiritual insights, and on and on. It's as if the parish world spins around them, and for them it does.

On a somewhat higher scale one might discover the cheerleader. I recall a piece by a colleague, Rev. Larry Alland, speaking about the season of Lent. He referenced a Creative Churchmanship Conference, a Women's Lenten series on the parables of Jesus, Sunday afternoon experimental worship, the solid Sunday morning attendance—all in the six weeks of Lent. He closed by saying, "This vitality is a reflection of the commitment to ministry you, as a member of the church, have made. Let's keep up the good work!"

Sometimes the "Minister's Minute," which unfortunately for a few years I called "Bowman's Aim," seeks to persuade folk in the parish to a certain point of view. I recall once I called attention to an upcoming Youth

Sunday in which the youth had helped to shape the liturgy. Seeking to appeal to adults, I wrote:

> You need to know some of what you have come to understand, but you need them to remind you of what you once knew, but have forgotten or cast aside. Both need God in order to learn what is not yet known.

Sometimes I tried to do serious theology in several paragraphs. One of these efforts appeared at the onset of Eastertide, April 1, 1970:

> Often at Easter we hear three commonly accepted myths which have infiltrated the teaching of the church: the myth of progress, the myth of the "immortality of the soul," and the myth of the hope of spring. All deserve a severe analysis. I can only suggest here.
>
> The notion of human progress is a fairly recent idea. It is doubtful if this is a biblical notion. "The Kingdom of God" is God's to bring in, as the Social Gospel preachers of the early 1900s learned to their chagrin. It is debatable as to whether scientific and technical progress humanizes us or ever brings us closer to God.
>
> In sermon and funeral orations, we have heard about 'the divine spark in man' or of the 'eternal essence' which cannot die. That is a purely religiocultural notion, not discoverable in the Bible. The New Testament teaches about death and resurrection to new life—a vastly different concept. Paul Tillich describes the Western myth of immortality as an escape from the "courage to be."
>
> To identify spring and Easter is to get all mixed up. T.S. Eliot said, "April is the saddest time of the year." He was right. It gives off a hope that is futile. We know winter is coming. There is no hope found in the "eternal return" of the seasons. On the contrary, Easter speaks of something brand new—a dramatic break-up of the certain slavery of death. Once—only once—death was not as certain as winter—and that makes all the difference.

## Worship as Experimental Experience

"There's no such thing as non-liturgical worship. There's either good or poor liturgy."

Raised in the evangelical tradition, I know casual forms of service. Those who prayed looked askance at formalized petitions. Rather they "opened their mouths to let the Spirit fill them." Yet, when analyzed, these casual prayers followed a formula that could find its way into print.

## Parish, the Thought

While at Park Church, from 1968 to 1971, much "experimental worship" developed around the country. In that local church, a good deal of restiveness manifested itself regarding the rather stiff and locked-in mode of the Sunday service. To some extent, sensing the desire for change, the Senior Minister, Rev. Ned Burr McKenney, in conjunction with the Board of Deacons, provided opportunity for new forms. In Lent of 1969 four alternative vesper services took place in Thompson Chapel. I provided planning and leadership.

The four services provided variety as follows:

1. A "Service for All Generations" included separate meditations for children, youth, and adults.

2. A "Sing-in for Peace" included a portion of a poem by the Jesuit priest, Daniel Berrigan. Convicted and sentenced for the destruction of draft files during the course of the Vietnam conflict, he then occupied a prison cell. The poem in part read:

    > A man stood on his nails
    > an ash like dew, a sweat
    > smelling of death and life.
    > Our evil Friday fled,
    > the blind face gently turned
    > another way, toward life.[2]

3. A "Folk Mass for Passion Sunday," taken from the Revised Liturgy of the Lord's Supper of the Episcopal Church, USA. Musicians at piano, bass guitar, and vibraharp accompanied the liturgy.

4. A "Drop-In Communion" for the first day in Holy Week presented the worship with a liturgy side by side with explanatory notes set for private reading. The printed meditation by Catholic author, Romano Guardini, led eventually to the printed invitation to come forward when ready to receive the loaf and the cup. The basic format of the service derived from the Iona Community of Scotland.

God is not better worshiped by some "high church endeavor on Main Street" rather than by a "low church" effort in a white frame sanctuary by the railroad track. Likewise, newness of form offers no panacea. Familiar forms may lead to dulled spirits. Some lively combination seems recommended.

---

2. Berrigan, *Testimony*, 174.

Liturgy may provide the comfort of the familiar and the adventure of the new. How desirable!

When two or three gather together, no matter the form, all seek the Presence.

## Doing Theology Regularly

The parish minister is ordained and installed as "pastor and teacher." So in the December 2003 newsletter at Bethel United Church of Christ, in Manchester, Michigan, I devoted the "Minister's Minute" to one traditional theory about the way the sacrificial death of Jesus applies to our sins: "The Son of Man came not to be served, but to serve, and to give his life a ransom for many" (Mark 10:45).

Old and current stories illustrate the meaning of "ransom" —The Norse myth of how everyone's tears might ransom Baldur from the dead; the account of *The Fisher King*, in which a guilt-ridden disc jockey risks his own life to ransom a derelict back from the brink of destruction; the C.S. Lewis space fantasy in which Dr. Ransom fulfills the meaning of his name by saving the mythic planet, Perelandra, from destruction.

The dying of Jesus on the cross has, in Christian theology, been called a "ransom offering." That is to say it is a price paid to redeem the people from aimlessness and sin back into the safety of God's eternal care.

The notion of ransom sacrifice finds a small place in many main-line Protestant pulpits. Yet how does Jesus Christ, as the United Church of Christ Statement of Faith says, achieve the "conquering sin and death?" Ransom is one way of answering that question.

We ask, "Does God demand the ransom?" and answer, "Yes." Immediately we add, "And God provides in Christ the ransom sacrifice." What God's moral law demands God's loving will provides. As in the story of Abraham and Isaac, God both requires and provides the sacrifice.

Once we attended an organ dedication in a near-by church. We sang these words from the hymn, "Salvation unto Us Has Come":

> And yet the law fulfilled must be, or we were lost forever;
> Therefore God sent His Son that He might us from death deliver;
> He all the Law for us fulfilled and thus His Father's anger stilled
> Which over us impended.

Well, it rhymes, but is there reason? These words, translated from a German source, Paul Speratus (1484–1551), contemporaneous with Martin Luther, remind us of the theology that made the little girl report to her mother about the church service, "Well, I like Jesus, but I don't like God."

I do, however, resonate positively with the next stanza of the hymn:

> Since Christ has full atonement made and brought to us salvation
> Each Christian therefore may be glad and build on this foundation.
> Thy grace alone, dear Lord, I plead Thy death my life now is indeed
> For Thou hast paid my ransom.[3]

Other hymns proclaim the ransom. For example, the hymn, "Praise, My Soul, the God of Heaven," reads as follows:

> Praise, my soul, the King of Heaven; to his feet your tribute bring,
> *Ransomed*, healed, restored, forgiven, evermore God's praises sing.[4]

It may well be argued that a key verse in St. Mark's gospel is, "For the Son of man came not to be served but to serve, and to give his life a ransom for many" (Mark 10:45).

## God

The rookie minister asked the veteran pastor, "About what should I preach?" The wise pulpiteer answered, "About God and about twenty minutes." That advice needs revision in light of contemporary short attention spans. The correct answer now is this: "About God and about twelve minutes."

In my first opportunity to speak from the pulpit on June 9, 1968, in Park Church, I chose as a title, "God." There issued from my lips a lengthy harangue taking up four printed pages. The paragraphs wandered about as with a person lost in the woods. Certainly the parishioners needed extra grace that summer's day to endure the so-called sermon.

It was Trinity Sunday. I sought to make this doctrine relevant. But only one illustration provided a window into the teaching. I related a story Cardinal Cushing of Boston told on himself. He was in a department store shopping. Someone rushed up to him, breathless, urgent, saying, "There's a man in the store seriously ill!" Immediately going to him and leaning over his prostrate form, the Cardinal asked, "My Son, do you believe in God the

---

3. Speratus, *Evangelical*, 314.
4. Lyte, *Lutheran*, 549.

Father, God the Son, and God the Holy Spirit?" The man replied, "Oh my, here I'm dying and he's speaking to me in riddles."

The human incident illuminated for a moment what I struggled to convey that day—that faith is a risk of a relational sort which allows the complexities of doctrine to await a more opportune time.

One year later, June 8, 1969, I mounted the Park Church pulpit again. Trinity Sunday. The message this Sunday consumed only one-half the previous time. The sentences strode forth in more Hemingwayesque fashion.

I began as follows:

> The greatest theologian of the twentieth century, Karl Barth, in 1928, said, "As ministers we ought to speak of God. We are human, however, and so cannot speak of God. We ought therefore to recognize both our obligation and our inability and by that very recognition give God the glory."[5]

Nevertheless, I sought to speak of God. Among others, I quoted American theologian, Roger Hazelton, who wrote:

> Traditional talk about a being who is supposed to preside over human affairs, whose prerogatives are properly described in the images of authority and sovereignty may of course persist for a long time in the church and elsewhere. But the well of conviction out of which these words and symbols arise is slowly, surely drying up.[6]

I spoke of the hidden aspect of God in some of scripture: portions of the Psalms, Isaiah, Job, Habakkuk, and Jonah.

In what I regard as a paragraph worth repeating, I said:

> What may the preacher say in this hazardous context? Probably what he has always said. Come. Be a believer. Take the risk of faith. God wills to be known even in his absence. Take the risk of fanaticism. The world's worst psychotic dreams have been acted out in God's name. The world's worst crimes have been committed for the sake of God. Take the risk of intolerance. Faith carries no guarantee of wealth, power, fame, or even friendship. Take the risk of self-righteousness. People still say to me, "I believe in God," as if some merit accrued to them on that account.

I feel it today, even as I felt it fifty years ago when I preached from the Park Church pulpit. People seem unbothered by the God question.

---

5. Barth, *The Word of God*, 186.
6. Hazelton, Roger, *Christ and Ourselves*, 8.

Atheists, such as Richard Dawkins or Christopher Hitchens, seem anachronistic. They struggle with believer's hangover. As Gabriel Vahanian, a French Protestant theologian, said in 1961:

> Modern man lives in a world of immanence. If he is the prey of anxiety, it is not because he feels guilty before a just God. Nor is it because he fails to explain the justice and love of God in the obvious presence of evil and injustice . . . Now man has declared God not responsible and not relevant to human self-knowledge. The existence of God, no longer questioned, has become useless to man's predicament and its resolution.[7]

I am not sure how many in the pews on that Trinity Sunday experienced the hiddenness, even the absence, of God. Perhaps the preacher spoke to himself and made an effort to find resourceful answers. How many times the person in the pulpit answers questions those in the pew do not ask!

I closed the homily titled, "God," by focus on the Christ figure, who has ever been my recourse. I said:

> The Christian way is modeled after one who, humanly speaking, risked it all and lost on the cross. "My God, why have you forsaken me?" It is to this figure that those of us plagued by the God question turn. In this time, when "something has happened in the consciousness of Western humanity," we must once again grapple with the one who said, "He that has seen me has seen the Father."

## A Sort of Forgiveness

Amnesty, a term garnered from the Greek, *amnestia*, meaning forgetfulness, holds slightly less weight than pardon. To pardon is to forgive, to say to someone or some group, as far as I am concerned you no longer stand guilty of the offense. Amnesty, on the other hand, relates exclusively to the punishment phase. It means to say, though you have acted in a wrongful fashion, I will pass over it and treat you as if it never happened.

An example of the dilemma faced by young men in the Vietnam conflict era appeared in a letter to "The Olympian," an Olympia, Washington, newspaper, sometime in the early 1970s as follows:

---

7. Vahanian, *The Death of God*, 147.

> I left America last on June 12, 1969, just four days after I graduated. It was indeed a difficult decision to leave the United States since I am an American citizen and love my country greatly. I have always tried to be loyal to my country and am proud of my citizenship. But for personal moral reasons I could not support the military role of my country in Vietnam. I applied for the status of Conscientious Objector but was turned down. After seeking counseling from some WSU staff members, I finally decided to emigrate to Norway rather than be drafted.
>
> Thomas V. Hansen
> Bankveien 9 F
> 1347 Hosle
> Oslo, Norway

Discussion of the issue swayed back and forth in the nation. President Nixon, continuing to prosecute the war, refused to countenance amnesty for those many thousands living above the border. A number of church and political leaders pressed for administrative action. The National Council of Churches Board adopted a statement calling for amnesty for all who were in legal jeopardy because of the war in Indochina, except those who had committed acts of violence.

On March 5, 1972, from the pulpit I took up this hot topic of U.S. men who had crossed the border to Canada or elsewhere in order to escape the jeopardy of the draft to service in the Vietnam conflict. My text, Matt 6:9-15, derived from the Sermon on the Mount in which we hear Jesus teach his disciples to pray, "and forgive us our debts as we forgive our debtors." (It's clear, since my topic was amnesty, that I ignored the nuanced difference between forgiveness and amnesty.)

In my pulpit word, I noted several objections to the fairness of forgiveness or amnesty. I asked, for example, "If I forgive my brother who has wronged me, how will that be fair to my brother who has not?" To put that in the public consciousness of the time, one might ask, "If I tell a U.S. citizen residing in Canada he can return to the USA without fear of legal repercussions, how is that just to the parents of a young man who obeyed the law, donned the uniform, and lost his life in a Vietnamese rice paddy?"

In response to that legitimate question, I pointed to the elder son in the parable of the father who had two sons, he who refused to be merciful toward his brother (Luke 15:11-32). I also pointed to the inclusive outreach to the south of President Lincoln following the Civil War, in order to "bind up the nation's wounds." I could have pointed to the reconciliation, led by Bishop Desmond Tutu in South Africa, in which the truth of Afrikaner aggression against the Coloreds, Asiatics, and Bantus, once confessed, received the amazing response tantamount to forgiveness or amnesty.

So I asked, "Can we find it within ourselves to receive in forgiveness those who have become legal outlaws? And who is going to grant them forgiveness for forcing them to decide between legality and conscience? Do we have to wait a century after the fact before we can respect acts of conscience?"

Picking up the topic in the next church newsletter, I referred to the phrase I learned from the ethicist, James Gustafson, about the church as "a community of moral discourse." Admitting that amnesty might well be a hot topic, especially for a minister less than one year into the life of the parish, I expressed satisfaction that I received few, "That's nice, Rev.," sorts of comments at the door, but found genuine dialogue instead. I knew I remained outside the advice of the Senior Minister, Rev. McKinney, when he told me, "I've learned never to say anything controversial from the pulpit."

On his second day in office, January 21, 1977, President Jimmy Carter, one of the most profoundly Christian men ever to occupy the White House, issued a presidential pardon to those who from August 4, 1964, to March 18, 1973, chose Canadian or other exile, or other options, over conflict in Vietnam. The pardon did not apply to the hundreds of thousands active duty military personnel who went AWOL or deserted during the course of the conflict. Thousands benefited from that action. Perhaps a volume of words from other pulpits, based on Matt 6:9–15, played some role in the President's action.

I realize that nowhere in that Sunday's discourse did I grapple with the conundrum featured in Reinhold Niebuhr's *Moral Man and Immoral Society*, namely that a straight forward moral act of an individual might not be readily available to a nation state. I note that such a caveat did not deter the good Baptist, Jimmy Carter.

On February 5, 1973, I spoke again at length on the call for amnesty. The Vietnam conflict was drawing to a close. I titled my pulpit word, "Let Bygones be Bygones."

In response, I received a gracious letter from an active member of the congregation, a World War II veteran. Virgil Michaelson noted the problems surrounding the Vietnam conflict but he insisted that if persons had fled to Canada or Sweden in the 1940s we might not have freedom now to discuss openly these sensitive issues. He spoke of his own "unbearable months" in Nazi prison camp. For those who avoided the call to serve, he was not willing to overlook it.

This respectful letter, concluded "in the Christian Spirit" it was intended, I still have in my keeping. This was an instance of the church as a "community of moral discourse" for which James Gustafson appealed. I do not have a copy of my reply. I hope it was as gracious as Virgil's letter.

## Mary Had a Baby

In my first parish, Park Church, in Grand Rapids, Michigan (1968–1971), talk about abortion galvanized a number of my colleagues. The Roe v Wade Supreme Court decision lay a few years off. The Senior Minister, Rev. McKenney, placed abortion advocacy petitions to Congress at the church door, appealing for signatures. My clergy peers were helping women find physicians who would perform abortions. I had no use for this activity.

When we came to Pullman, Washington, in 1971, I soon helped found a Pregnancy Counseling Center in Moscow, Idaho, the adjacent city. There I worked with Catholics and Protestants of similar views to enable girls and women to find a supportive atmosphere in which to find alternatives to abortion.

On December 10, 1972, I brought this issue to the pulpit in an oblique way under the title, "Mary Had a Baby." I wrote a dramatic dialogue for Mary and Joseph as they considered together the "problem pregnancy."

Taking extensive poetic license from the evangelists, Matthew and Luke, I presented the couple as caught in a struggle about what course to take.

The dialogue which Brenda Robinson, as Mary, and I, as Joseph, held that morning before the congregation took place as follows:

> Once coming to terms with Mary's pregnancy, they spoke of the threatening political circumstance around them—their poverty-laden situation and their forlorn hopes for Messiah. Mary exclaimed, "These circumstances grip me like a vise." Joseph even tells Mary he knows of a man who can end the pregnancy.

There is a pause, as if time has passed. Then the couple begin to speak to each other of the arrival of resources beyond themselves, "life affirmers" from the ancient text and saints around them. Mary tells Joseph she has "pondered things in her heart." Then she exclaims, "Dare I say it, Joseph. I feel as a co–creator of the world. Without me part of the future dies . . . Joseph, I feel that God is with me . . . I will have this baby!"

The dialogue builds in affirmation. Joseph exclaims, "Mary, we have traveled thousands of miles in this room. We can travel the rest of the way to new birth." And Mary replies, "Joseph, I feel the ecstasy of hope . . . I am literally inhabited by hope! My soul magnifies the Lord . . . "

So as Mary utters the words of the Magnificat, Joseph concludes it, words they both know from the tradition when Hannah bore Samuel, her first-born son.

In his excellent volume, *Psychology as Religion: The Cult of Self Worship*, Paul C. Vitz criticizes "selfism" psychologies that have attacked the family structure. He then offers a word of advice which I approve:

> May we not see that a psychologist advising abortion is acting in hostility against the deep structure of beliefs and meaning celebrated in the Christmas story? Recall that the young Mary was pregnant under circumstances that today routinely terminate in abortion. In the important theological context of Christmas, the killing of an unborn child is a symbolic killing of the Christ Child.[8]

Mr. Vitz sees the development of counseling approaches under the rubric, "family therapy," as a hopeful sign.

For a long time now I have noted that promoters of liberal thought in religion and politics speak out on behalf of the most vulnerable in society. They even say a society should be judged on how it treats its weakest members. How can they leave the fetus out of this equation? An anomaly!

Of course, I know the reply: "Well, the unborn is not yet a person." Really? How is it we allow nine allegedly wise persons to decide the arrival of personhood in the womb? What is there in our holy history that gives women, or men for that matter, "the right to choose"? We've come a long way, baby. A long way away from reverence for life.

## Funding Our Lives by Chance

During my last year of ministry in Pullman, Washington, and my first year in Tacoma, Washington (1981–1983), I filled the role of President of the Washington Association of Churches (WAC). I served as Vice President

---

8. Vitz, *Psychology as Religion*, 66.

previously (1979–1980). This body, the successor to the Washington Council of Churches, brought Catholics and Protestants together around many themes. Rev. Loren Arnett served for many years as its effective Executive Minister.

The ministries of the WAC were as long as your arm. It attended to refugees, food needs, employment, etc. Annually a legislative conference alerted churches to relevant issues on tap in the state legislature. The WAC supervised the Washington Wheat Campaign in which agriculture in the state contributed donated wheat to be shipped from Portland or Seattle to needy sites abroad. For example, in January 1984, 3,936 bags (200,000 lb.) of wheat traveled through Peru to Bolivia to be distributed by the indigenous churches to the most in need.

As I say, the vast amount of ministry would require many pages to disclose. Perhaps a report from Loren Arnett, in July of 1987, will serve to speak of the quantity and quality of the WAC's ministry:

- 250 refugees were resettled with the help of fifty-eight congregations.
- 360 refugees were placed in jobs.
- 281 Salvadorans and Guatemalans were provided emergency housing.
- $1.3 million worth of food passed through the Food Buying Service warehouse to food banks.
- 150 persons attended the Legislative Conference.
- Over 2,000 individuals and congregations received the legislative newsletter ALERT every week during the legislative session.

Stepping down from the Chair in 1983, I was appointed convener of a WAC *ad hoc* committee to study and report on private gambling and the proposed lottery in Washington State. At that time few states in the Union possessed state lotteries. The WAC advocated in the state legislature to keep a state-run lottery out of the picture. To no avail.

Not many in the churches knew of the millions of dollars in favor of the lotteries flowing into states from the gambling enterprises. Regularly newly designed games to entice the consumer came on board. Meanwhile, more and more church members found their way to Las Vegas or Reno to fritter away their God-given assets.

I well remember standing on a street corner with Rev. Paul Pruitt, a United Church of Christ minister and a member of the state legislature.

Earnestly he said to me, "I've not had one letter or phone call from any of the churches urging me to oppose the onset of the lottery in the state."

I think I have never heard a homily devoted to Christian stewardship in relation to gambling. I do have a record from the 1978 General Synod when Rev. Avery Post, President, UCC, said, "I do not want to bring people into our covenant on low demands, but as members we accept the stewardship of time and money . . . "

In the spring of 1975, in a series of pulpit words on social issues, I broached the subject of gambling. I said:

> Let's suppose two primitives meet for a first time in a clearing, with a bundle of fur skins over one's shoulder and the other with a basket full of grain on his head. Simultaneously, they think, "Exchange!" How might that exchange occur? One could by brute force or trickery rob the other. Or they might negotiate some sort of barter system. They might then make some sort of exchange based on a common, valuable currency. Who knows, they might even exchange gifts.

There is one more exchange possibility. I quote from the 1975 pulpit word:

> They could spot a piece of wood and throw it in a stream. If it comes down on the side with the bark showing, the pelts guy surrenders them all to the grain guy. If the non–bark side is up, then the pelts guy gets all the grain. It's an exchange. We call it gambling.

Gambling is a wild ride on the fatalistic back of chance. Exciting. Addictive. Also, antisocial and without any basis in reason.

One more element of concern enters. It's illustrated by my mother's refusal in my childhood to let me play marbles "for keepsies." She understood that such behavior loses the element of conscience. In the gambling act, there is a desire to win all, even if that leaves the other destitute.

In my homily, I weighed the pros and cons. Is not all of life, such as driving a car, a sort of gamble? Is not investment in the stock market a gambling behavior? Or is gambling not a benevolent behavior if public education receives a part of the proceeds? Or what if churches hold bingo parties to raise money for their operation? Even if gambling is an inferior sort of activity, may we not reuse the old phrase, "The devil's water being used to turn the Lord's mill"?

I countered these rationales with a central argument: the essence of the act is chance, and in this way lies outside the Christian's understanding of careful stewardship of resources. I noted that James Wall, editor of the widely-read periodical, "Christian Century," had been decrying the increase of gambling, a practice he found inimical to the tradition of the Christian faith and one that exploited the human temptation to greed.

I also argued that other human behavior that involves chance, such as climbing a mountain, involves all sorts of prudential, cautionary preparation. In gambling, all caution goes out the window, unless of course it involves "smart money" which is unethical on the part of the gambler.

In 1964, the State of New Hampshire introduced the public lottery to gain public revenue. Since then almost all states have fallen in line, many with inter-state lotteries. In New Hampshire, the state's road signs once read, "A lottery ticket is an ideal Christmas gift."

Is not the institution of state-sponsored gambling, with its increase in addictive behavior, one sign of a disintegrating civilization? And a practice enhancing such decline? And if a public service is worth supporting why not ask for it in the out-front mode of progressive taxes, rather than subtly out of the back pocket of weaker citizens?

Alas, the horse is out of the barn. Even to speak and write in the above manner seems quaint, does it not?

## The Gay Affair

In the Spring of 1978, in my seventh year as minister in Pullman, Washington, I undertook to bring to the Sunday morning pulpit four post-Easter messages on current social issues—gambling, abortion, homosexuality, and war. Nothing controversial about those, eh?

As it happened, the message on homosexuality fell on Father's Day. I am sure I noticed that. Convinced that human sexual activity and procreation go hand in hand, I saw no reason to shift the topic to another date. One woman in the congregation found herself quite upset that the subject matter coincided with the celebration of the male parent.

In a few words, let me summarize what I said from the pulpit. I began with allusions to a few of the scripture texts which reference the subject: Gen 19:1–29; Lev 18:12, 20:13, and Rom 1:18–28. I noted, too, those texts that lift up heterosexual relationships: Gen 1:23 (male and female in creation), John 2:1–11 (wedding in Cana), and Eph 5:22–33 (analogy on unity in the church to unity in male/female marriage).

## Parish, the Thought

I spent extra time with Rom 1:18–28. Paul's topic is idolatry. He asserts that those who bow to untrue Gods produce a darkening of minds. The turn to same–sex behavior becomes one of the expressions of some persons caught up in an idolatrous society. In this way, Paul seems to offer an implicit explanation as to why many homosexual persons do not feel this inclination is a matter of choice. Paul seems to speak of behavior modification by cultural influence.

I then turned to the arena of experience, though much, for better or worse, remained closeted in 1978. I referred to two persons. I mentioned Rev. Malcom Boyd, an Episcopal priest and writer, who had "outed" himself, noting that his book, *Are You Running With Me Jesus?*, had much good to say. I then quoted Rev. Nathaniel Guptill, then the UCC Conference Minister in Connecticut, who in public remarks, had argued that the aversion many people have to homosexual behavior probably should not be exorcised, "since it is a part of a system of sexual inhibitions that protects children from molestation by their parents and also sisters from their brothers, making intimate family life possible."[9]

I then began to become persuasive through reason. I argued for the civil rights of homosexual persons, without moving to the approval of the lifestyle. Loving elements appearing in gay and adulterous relationships need not lead to approval.

I appealed to folk to "test the spirits," so not to become swept along in tides of public opinion. I offered a quotation, growing out of what I called an "unfaithful spirit," from a passage in Sally Gearhart and William Johnson, *Loving Men/Loving Women*:

> As long as the church is able to perpetuate the belief that marriage and the family are the highest forms of human relationship it will be able to perpetuate itself as a heterosexual family–oriented institution . . . Heterosexual relationships and marriage as traditionally experienced are basically unhealthy.[10]

Under the "test the spirits" rubric, I referenced Thomas Maurer, a UCC minister and counselor, who argued that one's sexual choices should be viewed as no more value weighted than one's choice of cuisine.

I concluded with several propositions:

---

9. Based on personal notes at the occasion.
10. Gearhart and Johnson, *Loving Women*, 92–93.

- First, the need "to confess the fallen aspects of our own sexual imaginations and practices . . . seeking to bring them into conformity with the mind of Christ."
- Second, in civil society we need to oppose oppression and seek justice. In church we need to receive all persons on the basis of their Christian confession.
- Third, when it comes to the blessing or performing of same-sex unions in the life of the church, "we will decline courteously and firmly," regarding this not as a civil matter but a consideration subject to Christian discretion.

The denomination into which I was ordained in 1968, the United Church of Christ, drew me in part on the basis of its history of social activism, its defense of the powerless. In the past couple of decades, the epigram, "God is still speaking" (alleged to have been first uttered by that great theologian, Gracie Allen), appeared as the sum of the denomination's theories. In relation to the homosexual question, this meant that seven biblical passages, the natural law tradition and the advice of the historic church were inferior guidelines to the will of God when compared with the contemporary *zeitgeist*.

Once upon a time, I picked up the phone and called the UCC headquarters office in Cleveland, Ohio. I asked for the LGBT office. In a few seconds a male voice responded. We spoke courteously. Then I asked, "If I had called the UCC offices and asked for the office of traditional marriage, where would I have been referred?" He did not know. Now one should ask for LGBTQ, in order to be politically correct.

The UCC has prided itself on being the foremost mainline denomination in advocacy of the gay rights movement. A steep price has been paid. In 1957–1958 the UCC body came into being listing 2.4 million members. Now the claim is to 900,000 or so. The denomination's leadership has been willing to jettison its members not on the LGBT bandwagon. Its small new member growth in recent years, to a significant extent, came through accession of members from the Metropolitan Church, the gay/lesbian dominant denomination. Even this has not prevented the most momentous membership decline among the major Protestant denominations. And as time goes by, there's an effort to push the envelope. For example, now all sexuality education from cradle to grave is carried out jointly with the Unitarian-Universalist denomination.

Once, while Interim Minister at Bethel Church, I sat my confirmation class down to see a UCC produced film on the Amistad Incident, in which Congregationalists had played a virtuous and courageous Christian role. Much to my consternation, toward the close of the film there came a bit about the continual role of the UCC in its pursuit of peace and justice, including the gay rights movement in church and state.

As a matter of fact, the UCC denomination has gained a foothold on the pedestal it has chosen. If people hear of the UCC they think, "Oh, that's the gay rights church."

In 1998, four denominations approved a Formula of Agreement which enabled clergy in all four denominations to receive each other's ministers without much problem. As I write, three of those denominations—Lutheran ELCA, Presbyterian USA, and the UCC, have experienced horrendous internal spasms over the ordination of practicing gay and lesbian persons, the approval of which has caused massive loss of churches and members. The other body, Reformed Church in America, at its 2016 national assembly, once again refused to move out of its traditional posture.

With a few inclusions and nuances different, I would be pleased to speak from the pulpit today in the same manner I did in 1978. In the meantime, I have endured considerable ordeals, external and internal, which I will not elaborate upon here, over same-sex issues. One must confess that only God in wisdom knows the truth. Surely we see through a fragmented mirror and spy various images. I think the Catholic Church, with its ethical foundation in natural law, offers the best clues for clarity here.

I would add a pastoral note. Through the years, I have had opportunity to minister to practicing gay and lesbian persons. While I have held opposition to their lifestyle, I believe I have been enabled to treat them in the same manner as I would anyone else. Their response to me and my ministry indicates they felt treated well. I say this in credit to the Spirit, not to myself.

A lot of water under the bridge since the Spring of 1978. A whole torrent, in fact. The eddies in the stream had only begun to ripple. The deluge, now forty years old, was building. Now the flood is upon us.

## May 18, 1980—When Mt. St. Helens Blew

I had announced that for the all-church picnic in Reany Park the pastor had ordered a perfectly beautiful day. And so it was. Warm for May. Bright blue skies shone overhead as we gathered for morning worship. Afterward many of us stopped by our homes to don casual clothes and head for the park.

We had no idea that 300 miles to our west Mt. St. Helens had blown her stack. There had been plenty of advance warnings of the volcanic eruption. "Don't go there!" red zone parameters were established. Still, when she blew her top some fifty of God's children lost their lives. Others managed to outrace the hot ash and survive.

There we were playing games, conversing, preparing picnic food, and generally enjoying the day. Unaware were we that the mountain had exploded while we were in worship. At some point I looked to the west and saw a black line across the horizon below the cloudless sky. I said to my wife, Dianne, "That looks like the approach of a Midwest thunder storm."

Then from across the street, where he lived, the Lutheran Campus Minister, Roger Pettenger, hurried toward us. This is what I remember him shouting: "Don't you people know what's happened? Go home!" We did.

By late afternoon the ash, blown by the trade winds, had reached Pullman, Washington, on the Idaho border. It fell like a heavy grey snow. Unprecedented! Calm people became agitated. Nervous people reacted with patience. Public schools suspended classes. Washington State University (WSU) closed for the term, causing seniors to be concerned if they would graduate.

By the next morning two inches of ash lay on the Palouse hills. Some forty miles north, six inches fell and choked the winter wheat. Light like talcum powder when dry and heavy as cement when dampened. The scientists at WSU and at University of Washington could not agree as to the danger to the lungs of this ash, but there was a run in the drug stores on face masks. All seemed to agree that this ash bore real danger to internal combustion vehicles.

A week later, on May 25, 1998, my pulpit word title read, "Fall Out." It was Pentecost Sunday. I spoke of "ambiguous fall-outs" such as ash that clogs motors and injures lungs but might mix with the Palouse soil to produce fine crops. (This latter result indeed happened.) And then I called attention to "benevolent fall-outs" epitomized in the birth of the Church when the Spirit of God fell on praying and believing people empowering them to give unashamed witness to the Christ who brings wholeness into the world, a fall-out we still need. And then, in preparation for Holy Communion, I referred to the need for the bread to be broken in order to enter us. I used a quotation from the Jesuit priest, Daniel Berrigan, "When I hear bread breaking, I see something else. It seems as if God never meant us to do anything else . . . so beautiful a sound . . . the crust breaks up like manna and falls all over everything. And then we eat—bread gets inside humans."[11]

Then I prayed:

> O graceful fall-out from the Lord,
>> Covering us, getting inside of us,
>> with the flavorful nutrition of
>> amazing love.
>
> O graceful fall-out from the Lord,
>> spilling over the barriers
>> of our doubt and fears
>> with the fruit of divine favor.
>
> Spirit of the living God, fall on us.

I had a hard time living down my promise of a great weather day for a picnic—May 18, 1980.

## Easter Day in the Queens

When one says New York City, the name refers to five boroughs. If listed in terms of notoriety, in descending order, we name Manhattan, Brooklyn, the Bronx, Staten Island, and then Queens. Unfortunately, many people know Queens for a tragedy—the site of a horrendous rape and murder of Kitty Genovese while, as it is alleged, thirty-eight persons in neighboring apartments might have come to her rescue but failed to do so.

As of February 25, 1968, Rev. James H. Ameling had resigned as Associate Minister of Union Church, a formerly Congregational, now UCC, in the Richmond Hill section of the Queens. I was to assume that position as an Interim by the end of March.

Easter Day dawned on Union Church on April 14, 1968. A couple hundred persons or families bought flowers for the day in honor or in memory of a loved one. The choir offered up the anthem, "Lo, the Tomb is Empty," by Edward Broome. Then Rev. Arnold W. Tozer, the Senior Minister at the church since 1961, mounted the pulpit. As someone said, "If a Christian minister has nothing to say on that day, he/she should be quiet for the rest of the year."

---

11. Berrigan, *Love, Love*, 114.

The denouement of Mr. Tozer's message claims a fixed place in my memory. His title for the day, "Celebration," gives a clue that what ensued, though seemingly spontaneous, in reality grew out of his plans for the proclamation.

I recall with clarity that Tozer suddenly said something like this: "This is Easter. The day of Resurrection. Christ is not dead. He is risen. Why do you just sit there? Stand up on your feet. Shout 'Hallelujah!' Say 'Amen!' Give God praise and glory." As he spoke, his voice rose, his arms shot up, his whole being exuded animation.

Now this was no Pentecostal church. We were not in Baton Rouge with Jimmy Swaggert shouting, "My! My! My!", and then breaking into tongues. No, I refer to a staid and proper United Church of Christ in the heart of Queens.

What happened? The Easter congregation rose out of their gravely pews, all the while looking about for assurance. In a way there seemed to be no alternative, given the pastor's urging. But I can attest that from my seat in the chancel I saw not *proforma obligatory* obedience. There before my eyes, this old-line, main-line congregation stood *en masse* and shouted, "Hallelujah! Christ is risen. He is risen indeed." I too joined the celebration.

Not long after my Interim at Union Church ended, I, my wife, Dianne, and our young son, Kirk, moved on to a permanent situation in Michigan. But if someone asks me, "What's your most memorable Easter?", I suppose I might say, "Back in Queens when Tozer persuaded that congregation to stand up and shout, "Hallelujah!"

# Engagement Beyond the Sanctuary

I simply argue that the Cross be raised again at the centre of the market–place as well as on the steeple of the church. I am recovering the claim that Jesus was not crucified in a cathedral between two candles, but on a cross between two thieves; on the town garbage–heap; at a crossroad so cosmopolitan that they had to write his title in Hebrew and in Latin and in Greek (or shall we say in English, in Bantu, and in Afrikaans?); at the kind of place where cynics talk smut, and thieves curse, and soldiers gamble. Because that is where He died. And that is what He died about. And that is where churchmen should be and what churchmanship should be about.

George Macleod, *Only One Way Left: Church Prospect*[1]

---

1. Macleod, *Only One Way Left*, 38.

## Protest in the Heart of Grand Rapids: Baez and Harris Come to Park Church

By 1968 intense opposition to U.S. involvement in the Vietnam conflict spread across the land. Some of my colleagues and I found ourselves counseling young men concerning their relationship to military conscription, known as "the draft." If the local draft board proved sympathetic, a young man might escape being "called up" to this ugly war, especially if he could show evidence that his religious views led him to oppose war in general.

One young man in Park Church, experienced conscientious objections to the war but he had no personal record of conscience toward war. He felt it ethically dishonest, in face of an imminent draft, to lay claim to pacifism. He was the son of a mortician. His assignment? The mortuary on the battle field.

One day, Park Church received a request from folk singer, Joan Baez, and her husband, David Harris, to hold an opposition to the war concert in the sanctuary. It happened. I well remember the two of them walking into a packed house, she physically diminutive and he a towering figure.

But the decision to host the event at Park Church, across the street from Veterans Park, came only after much conversation and disagreement.

This account is based on my recollection of events. Maybe a recent conversation with Loyd Winer, Chair of the Board of Trustees at the time, is likely closer to the facts. He says that after the Trustees said "no" to the overture, the Custodian, Mr. Brodien, came to him saying, "I'm a black belt in karate. If there is any trouble I can handle it." So, Mr. Winer approached an agent for Joan Baez. It was agreed that if the agent would write a $5,000 check (no small change in 1969) to cover any property damage to Park

Church, the protest concert could proceed. When all came off peacefully, Mr. Winer returned the uncashed check to the agent. This is Mr. Winer's memory of the process.

Traditionally, Congregational churches had no central council or board, no hierarchy of decision making. Park Church inherited that tradition. Who then would decide whether or not to allow Baez and Harris to hold the concert in its sacred precincts? Surely the membership of the congregation at that time would not have held a homogenous view on the prosecution of the Vietnam conflict. What to do? This is how I remember it.

The Senior Minister, Rev. McKenney called the Trustees together. They voted by a narrow margin to disallow the event. Why? The ostensible reason involved fear of damage to the building, either from disruption inside or brick bats outside in the street. One must keep in mind the fact that pro and anti-war feelings ran high in those days.

The Board of Deacons also met. After all, they too had influence over events held in the sanctuary, the spiritual center of the church. After deliberation, the Deacons voted narrowly to allow the Baez/Harris protest event to take place.

What to do? Though I served as Associate Minister in the church, and one assigned with primary emphasis toward youth who soon would face the draft, Rev. McKenney gave me no invitation to attend these meetings. In an unusual process, the Trustees and Deacons came together for a joint decision. They concluded that as long as the sponsors of the event put up a bond, the protest concert could take place in Park Church.

As Baez and Harris swept into the right-hand front door of the church, I merely observed. But given the prominence of this folk musician and partner in the protest movement, one felt Park Church caught up in the current of the history of the time.

Why should the Trustees, apart from ideology or attitudes toward the "war," have been apprehensive? Central to their legitimate concern—the sanctuary windows. These twelve large, blue-toned, authentic Tiffany windows from the turn of the century were irreplaceable. How horrible to think of bricks or stones hurled at them, even though they were protected by translucent plexiglass. Any Trustee, given the time of protest and counter protest, might well have had second thoughts.

All took place in peace.

## Opposing War Selectively

In 1968, when I took up the role of Associate Minister at Park Church in Grand Rapids, the opportunity to preach from that ornate, uplifted pulpit from time to time presented itself. On August 11, 1968, I spoke from the text, "Give to the emperor the things that are the emperor's and to God the things that are God's" (Luke 20:25).

In almost defense attorney–like mode, I sought to present a Christian case for Selective Conscientious Objection to war. I argued in my opening sentence, "Mainstream Christianity has stood for the past fifteen centuries as a selective conscientious objector to war." I chose not to attack the morality of the Vietnam conflict *per se* or to take up the cudgels for the pacifist tradition in the faith. I claimed this text from St. Luke differs both from, "Resist not an evil doer" (Matt 5:39) and from, "Let every person be subject to the governing authority" (Rom 13:1).

The context in that moment included young men facing their local draft boards and seeking "conscientious objector" status from the ugly Vietnam war. Many boards took the stance that unless the alleged objector held conscience against all war their rejection of that particular conflict did not hold water, since that amounted to a political judgment, not a moral conviction about killing in general.

I noted that the tradition of selective objection to armed conflict in the history of the church found itself borne out in the situation at hand. I remarked, "It is fair to say that the large majority of organized resistance to the Vietnam War is not inspired by an ideological pacifism, but rather by specific moral objections to this particular undeclared and bloody war."

I continued to press the point. Is the only decision for a Christian person or community to salute and march off or to say, "By God, never!"? Pointing to the "just war" theory that grew up in the Catholic tradition, as distinguished from the vow of Stephen Decatur Jr., "Our Country! In her intercourse with foreign nations may she always be in the right; but right or wrong, our country!"[2] I invoked the German martyr, Dietrich Bonhoeffer, who forsook his pacifist stance to involve himself in a plot to assassinate Adolf Hitler.

The Old Testament reading for the day came from 1 Chronicles in which we learn that David, who wanted to build the temple, heard God say,

---

2. Originally Stephen Decatur, in an after–dinner toast of 1820. Later stated by, and often attributed to, Carl Schurz, 1982.

"You shall not build a house to my name, because you have shed so much blood in my sight on the earth" (1 Chr 22:8). Would God have been less displeased if David had shed less blood? Selectively?

In closing, I noted a statement issued by the World Council of Churches, meeting in Uppsala, Sweden, on July 16, 1968, enlisting the "spiritual care and support" of those in military action, as well as for those who found themselves conscientiously opposed to a particular conflict or who believed themselves under God unable to bear arms in any military campaign.

## On Being Selective in One's Service

During the late 1960s and into the 1980s the conflict in Vietnam caused the National Selective Service System to operate at full bore. Commonly known as "the draft," young men, eighteen years of age and older, were vulnerable to being "called up." Having registered as required, any day the letter might arrive indicating the recipient's number in the lottery had been drawn.

Given the nature of the conflict—its undeclared status and its questionable ethical legitimacy—many young people and their advisors sought to discover their status as possible "conscientious objectors" (CO).

During ministry in Grand Rapids, Michigan, I associated with colleagues in learning about the vagaries of the system. We learned that most draft boards demanded proof of a peace orientation prior to age eighteen, not allowing that as a "Johnny-come-lately" one could be a CO. We learned that some five-member draft boards frequently provided for CO status, while others scarcely ever did so. We learned about various avoidances of the draft, e.g., go to Canada, etc. With this and related knowledge we offered counseling. We became aware that having a background with "peace churches"—Brethren, Quaker, Mennonite—gave one an advantage in claiming CO status.

When arriving in Pullman, Washington, in 1971, this subject continued to demand attention. The Peace Discussion Group of the church joined in seeking to understand the Selective Service System "so that it might support people interested in the CO status "and others needing information as to their legal options" (Church Newsletter, February 1972).

Later on a local and tangible fulfillment of this learning process came to fruition. In 1973 a Conscientious Objector Committee was formed.

Working alongside the ecumenical Common Ministry on the WSU campus, we hired a young man to complete four months of his two-year alternative service term. Authorized by Lieutenant W. R. Orr of the Washington State Selective Service System, David Richard of Tacoma, Washington, came among us to do "facility improvement of churches" and "person to person work with local agencies." The nature of the work? "Community service."

In order to supervise David Richard's work, a committee—the Ecumenical Committee to Employ a Conscientious Objector—was formed, including persons from our congregation and other like-minded churches in the community. One newsletter from July 1973 stated that David "is hard at work on the third floor of Koinonia House, the location of WSU's Common Ministry." He worked on improvement of local church properties, volunteered at a convalescent home and engaged in several other community projects.

Those in the parish concerned about providing young people legitimate, legal options to actual participation in the Vietnam conflict found satisfaction in playing a role in fulfilling this objective.

As late as 1981 I wrote to the congregation saying, "I believe that American Christians need to take seriously the current registration of young men for an eventual draft. At their request Rev. Jim Nielsen, WSU Campus Minister, and I have been assisting high school administrators and counselors in refurbishing their knowledge about this matter . . . For Christian people the prospect of conscription and participation in war raises moral issues we may well help each other think through" (January 13, 1981, newsletter).

David Richard, where are you? I hope your work remains conscientious and community oriented. Thanks for being a witness to peace!

## "Good Morning, Vietnam!"

Certainly before, and afterwards as well, the expensive to treasure and blood conflict in Vietnam occupied our attention in 1972 and 1973. Serving in my second and third years of ministry in Pullman, Washington, adjoined to WSU, I was pleased to be located in a congregation that took seriously the social dimension of the Christian faith.

On January 4, 1972, I wrote in "The Communicator," the weekly newsletter from our congregation:

> Christian people everywhere cannot help but be reduced to profound sadness on account of the recent extensive bombing of North Vietnam. Some will find it necessary to defend this action as a necessary evil. I understand that rationale but I am not able to accept it for myself. Let each of us allow our thoughts/feelings to be influenced in depth by the truth as it is in Christ and then express ourselves in appropriate ways. Now is no time to be quiet. If we keep silence the rocks themselves will cry out.

Having come to the conclusion a decade earlier that I did not want to be associated with a denomination that hid out from the issues of poverty, racism and war, concerned only with personal piety, I at that time found the UCC a body amenable to a socially sensitive point of view.

Early in 1973 UCC President Robert V. Moss wrote: "My own view is that the U.S. Armed Forces should withdraw from Southeast Asia immediately only conditioned on the return of American prisoners of war." He urged UCC members "whatever their views" to communicate with the Nixon administration and Congress on the matter.

On January 17, 1973, "The Communicator" reported actions in support of a petition entitled, "Concerned Voters to End the War." We wrote to Representative Tom Foley, Washington State Fifth District Representative:

> The undersigned support this petition urging Congress to take a more active role in ending the Vietnam War. Specifically, we urge Congress to enact legislation terminating funding for military operations in Vietnam if a peace agreement is not signed by January 20, 1973.

The eight-member committee placed the petition at the entrance to the Student Union Building on the WSU campus in order to obtain further signatures.

One of my political heroes at the time, Senator Mark O. Hatfield, Republican from Oregon, addressed the National Prayer Breakfast on February 1, 1983. Seldom have pertinent prayer and proper politics been better welded together. In part, he said:

> If we as leaders appeal to the god of civil religion, our faith is in a small and exclusive deity, a loyal spiritual Advisor to power and prestige, a Defender of only the American nation, the object of a national folk religion devoid of moral content. But if we pray to the Biblical God of justice and righteousness, we fall under

God's judgment for calling upon His name, but failing to obey His commands.

We sit here today, as the wealthy and the powerful. But let us not forget that those who follow Christ will more often find themselves not with comfortable majorities, but with miserable minorities.

Today our prayers must begin with repentance. Individually, we must seek forgiveness for the exile of love from our hearts. And corporately, as a people, we must turn in repentance from the sin that has scarred our national soul.[3]

Senator Hatfield made no explicit reference to the Vietnam conflict. But when he spoke of "the sin that has scarred our national soul" there could not have been anyone in the room to mistake his reference.

Eventually the voices in the pews and the streets were heard. With agonized withdrawal the conflict ceased, but only after massive loss of life and treasure. The guns fell silent. From the silence came the sounds of sorrow.

## Clergy Day at Trident

The Naval Submarine Base Bangor, the west coast Trident nuclear submarine base, lies to the west of Seattle and Tacoma near Bremerton, Washington, on the Hood Canal. One day I received word that a "clergy day" would take place at the base to which we were all invited. I went.

I remember climbing onto a bus along with other clergy. Ironically enough, our tour guide proved to be a young Japanese–American officer. As we began to wind our way around the base he pointed out the wild turkey and the white–tailed deer inhabiting, what one could soon see, a piece of God's good earth worthy of national park designation.

Only one difference. Along the base road ran a continual fence of thick barbed wire. Then behind that a few yards another similar fence. And behind that, at regular intervals, turrets imbedded in the earth with large caliber guns projecting from the emplacements.

The tour continued. At length, we arrived at the center of the base where stood an impressive chapel and related buildings. We were introduced to five chaplains, each of whom occupied impressive offices staffed by his own private secretary. One had the impression that these chaplains felt they had reached the pinnacle of their religious profession

---

3. Hatfield, *Between a Rock*, 94.

We then were ushered into an auditorium where the captain of the base was introduced. He taught Sunday School each week, we were informed. He spoke to us about the base operation.

When the captain concluded his welcome and remarks, he asked for questions. I raised my hand and when recognized I asked, "If a chaplain on Sunday morning from the chapel pulpit were to raise some question about what goes on at this base, how would that be handled?" The captain did not hesitate. I remember distinctly to this day what he said. Matter of factly he replied, "That chaplain would be down the road the next day." So much for the Protestant tradition of freedom of the pulpit.

This incident confirmed in me a long-standing opinion that military chaplains, no matter how much good they do, are "kept persons." Just as journalists in the Afghanistan conflict "imbedded" with the troops on the ground where objectivity lost its grounding, so with the military chaplains. How much better for all concerned if the clergy were able to maintain their civilian identity, operating independently as did journalists during the Vietnam conflict, when the public received objective reportage.

During my ministry in Tacoma I participated several times in silent protest demonstrations along the Burlington Northern Railroad at the entrance to the base. These protests took place as train loads of parts entered the base to build or resupply the Trident submarines of genocidal potential. In leadership, James and Shelley Douglass, founders of the Ground Zero community, whose house was situated near that entrance. A noteworthy participant at times in these protests, Archbishop Raymond Hunthausen, Bishop of the Seattle diocese.

On a Sunday following the "clergy day" at the Bangor base, I used a good portion of the pulpit word time to tell of the clergy tour and of my repartee with the camp chaplain. During the discourse one of the church members rose from his pew and noisily walked out. I had conversation with him at his home in the week following. We agreed to disagree agreeably.

In his book, *The Nonviolent Coming of God*, James Douglass refers to a speech Seattle Archbishop gave at the University of Notre Dame, in which he said, "Our nuclear weapons are the final crucifixion of Jesus, in the extermination of the human family with whom he is one."[4]

---

4. Douglass, *The Nonviolent Coming*, 7.

## A Delegate to Synod

Representing the Washington–N. Idaho Conference, UCC, as delegate in 1977, I participated in the Tenth Annual Synod in Washington, D.C, and the Eleventh General Synod in Indianapolis, Indiana, of 1979.

Two memories stand out for me from the 1977 event. The first revolved around the apartheid situation in the Union of South Africa. What posture ought the Synod take in order to direct the denomination? Two major options appeared. One, take steps to join in the boycott of companies doing business in South Africa. Second, maintain church investment in some of those companies in order to attend Board of Directors' meetings there seeking to influence corporate policies. Significant arguments were advanced in committees and in the plenary sessions on both sides of the issue. The position to divest and join the boycott carried the day. In part, the synod resolved, "We now believe that withdrawal of business and investments from South Africa is a central expression of the Gospel witness."

The other issue memorable for me also swirled around race relations. Here's the substance of the matter: Rev. Benjamin Chavis, a UCC minister, was a part of the so-called Wilmington Ten charged with committing arson. At the synod, a march on behalf Benjamin Chavis took place advocating the freeing of the Ten. I clearly recall my role as a sort of "fellow traveler," inclined to support such movements but troubled that I never heard Chavis insist that he was innocent.

In 1980, Ben Chavis walked free from a thirty-four-year prison sentence after the Federal Appeals Court overturned the conviction of all ten and cited "prosecutorial misconduct."

Later on, Ben Chavis served as Director of the Million Man March. In 1993 he became Executive Director of the NAACP. His term in that office ended in 1994 midst reports of financial mismanagement.

At some point Chavis announced that he was both a Christian and a Muslim. The regional church body in North Carolina, where his ordination credentials lay, refused to renew his license for UCC ministry. It seems to me that my reservations about Ben Chavis were not exactly ill-founded.

In June 1979, I took my delegate credentials to the General Synod in Indianapolis, Indiana. Sexuality took a front and center role in that gathering. The Board of Homeland Ministries of the denomination published *Human Sexuality: A Preliminary Study*, which the synod received. At the same time a new group, the United Church People for Biblical Witness, published, *Issues in Sexual Ethics*, a response pointing out the misguided nature of the former document and etching out its own path. The floor of that General Synod rang with statements and rebuttals on the issues surrounding homosexuality.

Since that time, the so-called progressive policies on same-sex matters have gained ascendancy in the denomination. That trend has certainly hastened the decline in UCC adherents. Many persons and churches have left the body. More and more the denomination has declared its advocacy of the gay life—welcoming practicing homosexuals into its clergy, encouraging local churches to be "open and affirming," gaining membership by incorporating Metropolitan Churches into membership, and publishing all sexuality material in conjunction with the Unitarian-Universalists.

After 1979 Synods no longer featured fierce debates on the subject. The so-called progressives now held unchallenged sway. The dissenters had left for other pastures.

So, rather than being present at the creation, I would instead say I was present at the opening battles of the debate which has left the UCC a mere shadow of its former life. Present at the outset of the debacle.

In that same period of time, I attended a meeting of the Fellowship for Biblical Witness in Philadelphia, Pennsylvania. I came away knowing that not only was the mainstream of UCC thought on homosexuality out of step with my own position, but that the Biblical Witness folk were much too attached to scriptural fundamentalism for my own purposes. The UCC leaders too much misconstrued scripture. The Biblical Witness folk relied too heavily on a scattering of scriptural texts, failing to take sufficient note of the natural theology positions espoused in the Catholic tradition—a necessary adjunct in my opinion.

## An "Off the Record" Event

During my ministry in Tacoma, Washington, from 1982 to1988, I wrote a column for the religion page of the "Seattle Post-Intelligencer." My piece appeared every so often following pieces by five other ecumenical authors.

During that time, Pat Robertson, the TV evangelist, had thrown his hat into the ring as a Republican presidential candidate. One morning, opening the mail, I received a "Dear Brother in Christ" letter from the pastor of a large evangelical church in the Tacoma area. If I wished I could be included in an event at a Seattle hotel where Mr. Robertson himself would hold forth to gathered clergy in an "off the record" presentation.

Not a fan of Mr. Robertson, I tossed the invitation in file thirteen. Then an idea struck. Why not use my "in" with the Seattle paper to produce an interesting piece of news?

I picked up the telephone. I said, "How would the religion news office like to attend an "off the record" event with Pat Robertson? Only a few minutes later the call came back. "Yes. When?"

So, early in July 1984, Mary Rothchild, Religion Editor, and I met at the entrance of said hotel. She walked in with me as if she were one of the designated clergy for the occasion

We sat for a while. Then the emcee said Mr. Robertson had been delayed so perhaps we would like to sing some choruses. We sang. I knew none of the songs as they were from the evangelical side of the house, distant from my own environment. Finally, the man of the hour arrived.

Mr. Robertson is one of those glib fellows who has no need to think before he opens his mouth to speak. I have no recollection of what he said, but we were assured that it was hush-hush material not for the consumption of a general public in less discriminating earshot. Meanwhile, Mary, the religion news editor, took assiduous notes.

Outside the hotel, the press had gathered. When Mr. Robertson emerged, he held a question and answer time for the reporters. Mary Rothchild attended that event as well. She walked away with the inside dope and the public news.

Soon afterward, under Mary's by-line, came a fascinating piece in which she reported the not always congruent inside and outside news. The editors must have regarded it as something of a scoop since it found a place on the front page of the newspaper.

Did I take inordinate pleasure in the subterfuge? Yes.

## Meeting a Press Deadline

While writing for the "Seattle Post-Intelligencer" (PI), one incident of importance, and somewhat humorous, sticks in my mind.

In that era, Jim and Tammy Faye Bakker held forth on television's Trinity Broadcast Network, carried on six thousand television stations and reaching five million households every week. In 1987 the scandal broke, revealing the Bakkers illegally pocketed income from the program and life in palatial luxury. They even trimmed their dog's house in gold.

A piece I wrote for the PI follows, published on July 4, 1987.

## Engagement Beyond the Sanctuary

The father of the bride sat across the rehearsal dinner table. He asked, "Has this Jim Bakker scandal caused any problems at your church? "No," I replied, "just a few good laughs." He looked puzzled and pointed out what a great tragedy it all is. Trying to bring myself to that point of view, and visualizing, in particular, those whose faith was shaken by the whole miserable thing, and drawing in my mind's eye the scenario of some widow laying aside and mailing a sacrificial greenback in response to a teary-eyed plea for support, I found it possible to agree. "A tragedy, indeed."

But the truth is, for years now some of us have discovered the TV evangelists to provide an endless source of humor. When the mind refused to be any longer creative at the end of the day, one could flip on the cable channel and readily find any number of guffaws right at hand, and in one's own field of expertise. Now with the revelations of dalliance, opulence, and indulgence, all this source of humor seems threatened.

But, I hear someone insist, "Are these scandals not injurious to the church?" Perhaps. But are we sure TV evangelism is constitutive of the church? What is church? The old Lutheran answer comes readily: "The church exists wherever the Word is rightly preached and the Sacraments correctly administered." Well, the TV extravaganzas must be something other than that. The old Congregational tradition said: "The church exists wherever true faith community may be found." Once again the definition ill-fits. If, "Christ takes form in a band of persons," then how might he find shape and substance through images in isolated living rooms and dens?

Or someone may say, "The church exists where time, talent, and treasure are pledged and shared in a common bond of faithful stewardship." What, I ask, can this possibly have to do with "sending in a pledge so your family will prosper" or "filling in a check to keep some evangelist alive" or "making a contribution so you can receive in book form the twelve answers to life's great questions?" Nothing, I think.

Proverbs 16:18 reads, "Pride goes before destruction, and a haughty spirit before a fall." Never has the sacred text been so infallible. The religious media empire, built on hubris and hype, now falls apart like the proverbial house of cards. My mother told me, "Never laugh at someone else's expense." But, Mom, it's hard to hold back a bit of a chuckle when a braggart religious spirit falls on hard times.

"But don't you imagine the Bakkers, et al., will rise again?" Yes. Probably. Memories are short. And to quote another proverb from that evangelist of the circus tent, P. T. Barnum, "A fool is born every minute." So look for TV evangelism to survive the crisis and come rolling back with even greater success. That may not be so great for the church but it's hopeful for those of us who find there moments of comic relief.

Actually, I do see a tragedy of sorts here. There is a lot of spiritual hunger around. It's fertile soil for various religious enthusiasms. Note the "New Age" movement as a case in point. One can even read of this tragedy in scripture, "For the time will come when they will not stand wholesome teaching but will follow their own fancy and gather a crowd of teachers to tickle their ears" (2 Tim 4:3).

I hear someone else saying, "There's an altogether too smug and self-righteous tone here." I agree. Special prayers are needed for those who write and publicly say prayers. Did not the missionary, Paul himself, worry about becoming a "castaway," a religious derelict? So while flipping the channel, a small prayer, please, for this all too vulnerable writer.

P.S. I wrote the above in the mid-eighties. Now here we are in 2017. Tammy Faye, bless her well-mascaraed soul, is no longer with us. But Jim, exited from prison, is back on the "telly" huckstering his prosperity gospel as if nothing nefarious had happened. Is that not a sort of bizarre, inverse witness to the Resurrection?

## The Scarlet Pimpernel in Clergy Garb

Just twice in my life I laid eyes on Daniel Berrigan. Well, at least once. The first time took place at a Fellowship of Reconciliation (FOR) gathering in Washington State some time mid-seventies. He had been arrested in August of 1970 at a hideaway on Block Island, Rhode Island, on the property of the lawyer, William Stringfellow. At the sighting I describe, he must have completed his three-year sentence for burning 378 draft board files in Catonsville, Maryland, on May 17, 1968.

If memory serves, he was again on the lam. Perhaps for some other non-violent civil disobedience in protest of the Vietnam War. There I sat among other FOR members and fellow travelers. Then there he was on stage, a slight, wiry fellow appearing without ceremony, like a puff of smoke. He spoke. I have no memory of what he said. Then, as suddenly as he appeared, he was gone. A fugitive from the FBI. A witness of courage and daring against the illegal, immoral, venture of the USA in Southeast Asia.

## Engagement Beyond the Sanctuary

Thinking back on that occasion, I am reminded of the Scarlet Pimpernel, that iconic figure from the French Revolution. Of him they wrote:

> They seek him here, they seek him there
> Those Frenchies seek him everywhere
> Is he in heaven or is he in hell?
> That demned elusive Pimpernel.[5]

Surely this speaks to the experience of the FBI often frustrated in its attempts to corral Berrigan. Director J. Edgar Hoover sought him and put him on the Most Wanted List. Still he appeared in a pulpit or on a television show and then evaporated out a back door in the custody of those providing him with a safe house here and there.

I saw him only one other time. I was in Berkeley, California, attending the Earle Lectures at the Pacific School of Religion. This would have been some time in the eighties while I served as minister of the UCUP, Tacoma, Washington. I hurried along a business section sidewalk with coat lapels turned up against the wind and rain. Suddenly a slight figure flashed by on the left, between the store wall and me. There and gone. "That was Dan Berrigan!" I muttered in surprise.

Of course, I could be wrong about this second meeting. No introductions. No speech. Just a visual sighting. One piece of circumstantial evidence. Reportedly he served on the faculty of the nearby Jesuit seminary. "Scarlet Pimpernel," hurrying by in the rain. It made my day.

Daniel Berrigan
(1921-2016)
Prophet, poet, peacemaker.

---

5. Orczy, *Pimpernel*, 114.

# Mission to the World

The Church of Jesus Christ is not basically a group of people who have gathered themselves together like a neighborhood improvement society to solve a common problem; nor is the church essentially a friendly gathering of congenial and like-minded people, who meet at agreed-upon times to enjoy one another's company. At its very beginning, the church was more like those who come together in answer to a fire alarm . . .

Loring D. Chase, *Words of Faith*[1]

---

1. Chase, *Words of Faith*, 61.

## Bringing Amistad Home

I HARBOR NO RECOLLECTION in my public school acquaintance with United States history of hearing about the Amistad incident. Checking the index of Howard Zinn's, *A People's History of the United States, 1492-Present*, no reference to the incident appears. Surprise! Given the sorry history of black-white race relations on this continent, one would expect this piece of history to appear. Indeed, when author, Bernice Kohn, in 1971, wrote *The Amistad Mutiny*, she was "surprised to discover how little information there was on the Amistad incident . . . "[2] (The following narrative draws on her reportage, supplemented by information found in Wikipedia.)

So it came as a surprise when the offices of the UCC began to help our recall. Indeed, it is said that the American Missionary Association (AMA), the outreach arm of Congregationalism in this country, emerged in response to the emergent need of Amistad slaves. (The AMA was a predecessor to the Board of Homeland Ministries of the UCC.)

In a nutshell, the incident began when fifty-three Africans from Sierra Leone were captured and enslaved on the Spanish slave ship, "La Amistad," which ironically means "friendship." Cinque, the leader, and his slave companions, mutinied, intending to return to Africa, but not knowing how to navigate, they ended up off Montauk, the tip of Long Island, New York. Cinque and his followers were captured and jailed in Connecticut, accused of piracy and murder.

The slaves spoke only Mendi, their native language. Who would have facility to defend them? Lewis Tappan, a New York merchant, found Rev. Joshua Leavitt and Rev. Simeon S. Jocelyn, who formed a committee to

2. Kohn, *Amistad*, book jacket.

raise funds for the defense of the prisoners. Professor Josiah Willard Gibbs, a teacher of theology and literature at Yale College, found James Covey, a Mendi, fluent in Mendi and English, as translator. Professor George E. Day taught the prisoners English and instructed them in the Christian faith. By that time the case had reached the U.S. Supreme Court. Retired President John Quincy Adams, famous for his dedication to the cause of abolition, was persuaded to defend the captives. On February 24, 1841, he rose to his feet before the court. He experienced a "grateful heart for aid from above." He spoke for four and one-half hours to the judges and auditor witnessing no flagging of attention. In closing, he warned the judges that they would one day stand before a higher court and would want to hear, "Well done, good and faithful servant; enter thou into the joy of the Lord."[3]

On March 9, 1841, the judges handed down their decision. Freedom! For Cinque and his companions a funded door opened for them to return home. On November 27, 1841, they set sail.

Amistad II, a traveling exhibition of African-American art created between 1790 and 1975, came to WSU through the liaison of our congregation, Community Congregational, in Pullman, Washington. It was displayed in the WSU museum, February 3–23, 1976. While there 4,339 visitors viewed the exhibition. Grant Spradling, Coordinator for Art, UCC, New York, visited. He commented, "The showing here was undergirded by the finest community support and involvement I have seen anywhere." Our stalwart church members, William Moseley (African American), Carl Stevens, Marjorie Grunewald, and others made this possible.

Over fifty artists' pieces, covering a wide diversity of styles, appeared in Amistad II. The exhibition included the water colors of Jacob Lawrence. Among the best known of twentieth century American painters, he featured portrayal of African American life. His sixty-panel migration series depicted the movement of African Americans from the rural South to the urban North. In 1970, he came to the University of Washington in Seattle, Washington, as a professor of art, where he remained until his death, June 9, 2000.

About half-way through an eleven-year ministry in Pullman, Washington, I found it pleasing to be a part of a local and wider church whose concerns included the historical incident of human freedom and the exhibit that artistically honored that memory.

---

3. Ibid., 85.

Parish, the Thought

## On a Wing and a Prayer in Puerto Rico

During the Spring of 1969 a group of 136 high-school-age young people, chaperoned by thirty-three adults, departed Grand Rapids, Michigan, winging their way to San Juan, Puerto Rico. The purpose was mission, not fishin'.

The group assembled from four Grand Rapids churches—First (Park) Congregational, Second Congregational, East Congregational (all United Church of Christ bodies), and Westminster (not Westminister as nearly everyone called it) Presbyterian. Their purpose: a week of work camp in Puerto Rican sites related to the two denominations.

The clergy leaders, all four in their early years of pastoral ministry, were Rev. John Kerr, Rev. Gil Miller, Rev. Bob Baker, and yours truly.

Prior to embarking on this mission adventure these four journeyed to the island to scout out the land and touch flesh with the local church leaders. We flew on some decrepit air bus labeled Pioneer Airlines. John Kerr recalls that Gil Miller was as "nervous as a cat on a hot tin roof" and was thoroughly soused by the time we landed. Certainly this scouting expedition proved to be an essential ingredient in the success of the mission trip.

The young people and their chaperones performed a variety of tasks: Shoveling gravel for a new road, laying cement, painting buildings, etc. Often there were significant interactions with the local people. The meals we shared usually consisted of chicken gizzards, rice, and guava juice.

A peculiar element of memory involves the many incidents forgotten and the few that remain from long past activities. One of these retained memories involved the leader of the church site at Yuquyu. In conversation, she complained about the inroads made by Pentecostal ministries upon Roman Catholic and the UCC members, syphoning off members into their fold. In the same conversation, she explained the absence of her husband. "Off on a mission for World Neighbors," she said. He, who while praying, had experienced what he believed to be the gift of the Holy Spirit in the speaking of tongues. She did not seem to sense the irony of these two pieces of information delivered to me in one conversation.

Another piece of memory involves Laurie. An outgoing, attractive young woman, she magnetized the young men surrounding our Yuquyu site as honey draws flies. I had been warned that the young men could be quite aggressive with their attentiveness to young women. So when I saw several of the guys, and especially their somewhat older leader, in animated conversation with Laurie, who responded openly, I felt apprehension rising in me! I needed to protect the brood and the fox hovered near the premises. Fortunately, nothing untoward developed.

Some years after leaving that ministry I learned, to my deep sadness, that Laurie had taken her own life. Some other fox intruded and the protection failed. What a loss!

This work camp, along with later annual trips, formed a bond that persisted through the years. One member of the group recalls high school as an unwelcome experience, relieved by the bonding known in the Pilgrim Fellowship, the church youth group. Today a core of those folk, now grandparents, keep in regular touch on Facebook. The comradery that grew from such trips, "The best thing that ever happened."

## Youth Work Trip and a Surprise

My role at Park Church focused on youth. That included the tradition of a "work camp" somewhere far from the local precincts, usually taking place during spring school break.

Following the extravagant four-church trip to Puerto Rico in 1969, two more such ventures took place. In 1970, four adults led twenty-three "Pilgrim Fellowship" youth to inner-city Chicago for study and altruistic labor. Of that trip, for some reason, I have no recollections at all.

In 1971, our expedition took us to UCC ministry locations in South and North Dakota. We divided our team for efficient use of time and energy. One-half journeyed north to White Shield, Fort Berthold Reservation, to associate with and work among Arikara/Sahnish, Mandan and Hidatsa people. The other half settled at Red Scaffold on the Cheyenne River Reservation, among Dakota people. There we improved a meeting house and renovated a parsonage.

Loyd Winer, who headed up the Red Scaffold work group, entertains several memories of the occasion, most having to do with his own initiative. First, discovering the dilapidated condition of the outdoor toilet, he persuaded someone to allow the group usage of the nearby school facilities. Second, as a licensed professional engineer (an expertise we were fortunate to have on board), he found a way to obtain a permit and materials to electrify the meeting house they were there to improve. Third, the Indian women provided a wonderful end-of-the-week meal, but first he had to visit the hardware store to replace blown fuses and broken bulbs. Loyd says, the women "were so happy it was beyond belief. It was like God turned them on. The Chief's wife gave me a homemade quilt as a gift of thanks. I felt bad about taking it, because I understood she lived in a cabin with a dirt floor. I still have the blanket and think of her when I look at it."

Certain moments in time stand out for me from the Dakota Trip:

- Driving across the empty countryside of South Dakota reservation land and feeling the ghosts of bison herds and native encampments ...

- Riding in a bus with an educated, young Dakota woman and listening to her describe two issues: the tension between leaving the reservation to join the "white man's world" or staying in order to assist one's own people; the fact of the simultaneous discovery of lively newness and the loss of traditional knowledge, e.g., when the English language enters, the survival of the native tongue becomes threatened ...

- Sitting in a church hall beside residents of White Shield, wanting to get acquainted. Aware of the silence in the room, not a quietness of hostility or exclusion, but the silence of "We don't do much small talk." Then silence spoke to me saying, "Words have weight. We don't go in for aimless chatter ... "

- Complaint over loss of sacred burial sites in the construction of Garrison Dam ... [4]

On Sunday, May 2, back at home, our group led the morning worship. Elements of the service included an "Indian Version" of Psalm 23, readings by youth from Vine De Loria's, *Custer Died for Our Sins*, and reports by participants in the two locations.

One event of immense proportion grew out of the Dakota venture. The pastor and spouse at Red Scaffold approached me privately. They simply said, "Our fourteen-year-old daughter, Elaine, is eight and one-half months pregnant. Serious tension exists between the father's family and ours. There is a threat of violence. Will you take Elaine back with you and allow the child to be born in Grand Rapids? All this until things cool down."

Startled by the request? That barely says it. Discussion with our group leaders raised a number of caution flags. What if she doesn't want to go? What if she goes into labor on the way to Michigan? What if her husband

---

4. The Three Tribe area originally comprised 12 million acres; Congressional acts reduced it to 3 million acres. The Garrison Dam, begun in 1946, reduced the Three Tribe area to 500,000 acres. The native peoples lost 94 percent of their agricultural lands. The peoples, in 1949, finally received a compensation payment of $7.5 million, far below a legitimate price (North Dakota State Government information documents).

tries to follow her to Michigan? How would we finance the delivery, hospitalization, child care, and post-partem care for the mother? But it was one of those few moments in life—and I hesitate to say it—when I felt God's thumb in my back. We did it.

Elaine moved into the parsonage with us. Dianne, my wife, already much too busy with our three young children, took charge with usual skill. She had assented to the project but the actuality presented many demands.

A major concern: Elaine scarcely spoke. This because she came from silent people. This, too, because she waited with people strange to her. One can imagine angry feelings from being removed from her people and "shipped off" to a "foreign land." But one evening, as if a light came on, she began to talk. Not about mundane things, but of mythic tales, creatures running and flying, and portents in the sky.

Elaine gave birth at Butterworth Hospital, Grand Rapids, where our two daughters had been born. Dianne, the next thing to a midwife, sat at her side. Elaine gave no visible sign of pain or discomfort during the course of her labor. All went well.

After three months' time, Elaine returned to Red Scaffold. For some years we stayed in touch. She named her second child Kirk, the name we had given our son. She voiced appreciation, as did the family, for the help and hospitality. Then as time passed we lost touch. Even now I wonder how Elaine and the child fared. I hope and pray the road evened out. But life on the reservation is not easy. Ghosts of the past still haunt and everyday realities remain harsh.

Evaluation of work camps for youth far from home yields a mixed bag. On the one hand, trips usually journey to a deprived setting. Surely the young workers get a splash of reality in their faces. Further, they do engage in an altruistic volunteer effort. Sometimes, though not often enough, they work side by side and become acquainted with indigenous young people. On the other hand, the contributors may emerge seeing themselves as more philanthropists rather than sacrificial givers. Also, only a limited amount of work rolls out in one week. And such events may increase the sense of dependency in the recipients. Even worse, the indigenous folk imbibe an increased sense of a far off favored group of people of whose status they may only dream.

Overall, for better or worse, these sorts of trips take place, with full planning on both ends of the effort. The providers and the recipients must see enough value to overcome the deficits.

## The German Adventure—1985

### *Kirchengemeinschaft*

The Evangelical and Reformed Church that joined with the Congregational Christian Churches in 1957–1958 to form the UCC possessed historic ties to the *Evangelische Kirche der Union* (Evangelical Church of the Union—EKU). In 1980–1981 the UCC declared *"kirchengemeinschaft"* (full partnership) with the EKU of the German Democratic Republic (GDR/East Germany) and Federal Republic of Germany (FRG/West Germany).

Based on those old and renewed ties a plan evolved to send four persons each from Maine and Washington/North Idaho Conferences, on a visitation to the related churches on both sides of the wall in Germany.

In the summer of 1985, I received an invitation from Conference Minister, Rev. Jim Halfaker, to be one of the representatives. When I requested permission to be away September 10–October 11, I noted to the church board my 1984 attendance at the Barmen Convocation at the University of Washington (a study of the Confessing Church in the 1930s) and at Garrett Evangelical Theological Seminary, a colloquy called, "The Church's Influence on Disarmament Decisions East." I expressed hope that I might not only represent the church but also bring back insights of value to the congregation.

When I think of the month in the two Germanies a kaleidoscope of images pour through my mind. What I do here is to share in verbal form a few of these memories.

Our German visits featured meeting and conversing with pastors and laity of the EKU churches. Rev. Jean Bass, a UCC pastor from Maine, and I early on reached Leitenau, a few minutes southeast of Paderborn. We were wined and dined by Rev. Peter and Ursala Missfelt. Later that day we were joined by Rev. Norbert and Renate Rompler, our key people for the visit in that area. Herr Rompler served an urban church in heavily Catholic Paderborn, serving university, business, and professional people. Impressive people! Ursala had once worked for Professor Werner Kümmel in Marburg and provided some assistance to Professor Rudolf Bultmann.

On the evening of September 15, we gathered at the Missfelt home. Joining us a Mr. and Mrs. Gunnel, he a successful manufacturer of auto parts and she a considerably younger woman who had no skill in English. The Romplers came, as did a number of other members of the parish.

Pastor Missfelt had told me to go after peace and justice issues in our conversation. He said, "If you don't do it, it will just be light talk." So, with wine glasses poured and after a toast, Pastor Missfelt introduced the subject and turned us loose. I suppose you could say I was "loaded for bear" and I fear gave off some ugly American signs. I spoke of raising peace related themes in my home pulpit. I spoke too of muzzled, pampered chaplains at the Trident Nuclear Submarine Base near Bangor, Washington. Jean Bass, my colleague, had other agendas, and I felt by the body language of Peter Missfelt that I may have been too assertive, though the next day his cordiality belied those fears.

Later, on Monday evening, September 17, members of the parish of St. Lukas, Paderborn, gathered in the Rompler's ample living room, twelve of us all together. It was a time when, as my colleague, Rev. Larry Alland, used to say, there was "much speaking to be understood and listening to understand." Again, on the subject of peace with justice we shared with a bright group reflecting various political leanings, all with backgrounds of considering the options.

It seemed clear that such conversations did not characterize the EKU there in Rhineland or Westphalia. We broke new ice in parish dialogue. The presence of these Christians from the USA, combined with the risk taking of the Missfelts and the Romplers, enabled an evening of lively conversation. Frau Rompler, when we were alone, said to Jean Bass and me, "Your coming has been a real win for our community." I knew then that we both stood on the shoulders of Rev. Frederick Trost, the then Conference Minister in Wisconsin, and others, who enabled these exchanges to take place.

## The Venture to Germany

Though we viewed some sights, this carried no intention of a sight-seeing expedition. Our purpose: to bring the greetings of the churches of our respective UCC conferences and to address common concerns, especially peace and justice.

We divided our time between West and East Germany. What a marked contrast! With the aid of the Marshall Plan the industrious West German people recovered from the Hitler years and then worked an economic miracle of their own. Waking early, one could hear the hum of vehicles on the autobahn headed toward office, field, or industry. We had every sense of entering a prosperous thriving first-world situation.

When we entered East Germany, the other side of the wall, the contrasts struck us immediately. Perhaps the first awareness of difference came in the air we breathed. Dirty! The Marxist government kept assuring the populace that the atmosphere improved. Nobody believed it. Grimly, they joked about it.

The cause of the filthy air? "Brown coal" obtained from earth stripping operations. One of the pastors took me on a surreptitious jaunt out into the countryside to see the mining in progress. In so doing he broke the rules. Stealthily, we stopped, watched, then silently motored away. Should we have stopped by a brook or small river we would have seen waters clogged, appearing to gasp for air.

A walk along east of the wall urban, commercial areas left indelible impressions. Empty showrooms and shelves? No. But a problem. Lots of goods which most of the population could not afford to buy. I remember especially kitchen and washroom appliances filling to overflowing the stores, but not many shoppers. The system did not operate by supply and demand. Over supply and small demand.

In West and East we found equally warm welcomes in parish halls and homes. One difference worth comment emerged. There existed greater willingness in the East than in the West to speak of the days of the Third Reich. Why? In all areas grandparents and parents of those who greeted us may have been implicated in problematic behavior. But in the eastern region the Marxists urgently portrayed themselves as the conquerors of the Fascists. I distinctly remember an experience in East Germany when we, along with hundreds of school children, were ushered into an auditorium to view a propaganda film portraying the communist victory over Hitler and his henchmen.

One thinks of the relative strength of the churches East and West. It was Rev. Martin Niemöller, Nazi resister, who once observed, "There is more genuine church life in Communist East Germany than in the West where it "has suffocated in prosperity."[5] I saw evidence of that strength and courageous faith east of the wall.

A noteworthy difference in regard to church and state in Germany versus the USA centers in taxation. At that time, in 1985, the church on both sides of the wall received approximately 10 percent of the taxes to

---

5. Niemöller, "Current Biography," 302.

carry out the work of welfare and benevolence in society. We saw in the west a wondrous community in Bethel where existed a large center for living and constructive work for variously disabled persons. In the East, the tense situation between church and state to some extent lessened due to the benevolent welfare the church carried out in all sectors of society.

Certainly, in the West and East we encountered pastors of intelligence and commitment at work in the vineyards of the Lord, each facing distinct obstacles, the prosperous secularity of the west and the atheistic regime of the East.

The following essays with anecdotes offer the reader some of the salient features of the four weeks we spent in Germany in the fall of 1985 under the auspices of the UCC.

## In Frau Marianne's House

Our hostess, Marianne Goebblesmann, lived in Hasslinghausen, a town said to contain 12,000 citizens—9,000 Protestant and 3,000 Catholic. (They always seemed to have the distinction in mind.)

Her grandfather and grandmother, a Jewess, left Russia during the Revolution. They were killed in World War II concentration camps, but Marianne's mother was hidden by friends in Hasslinghausen, in part because her husband was such a faithful physician.

Our stay there included a visit to the nearby church in Barman which hosted conversation in 1934, out of which came the Barman Confession. In spite of its equivocation on the Jewish plight, the statement remains a sign of courage and faith in its time.

Jean Bass and I were treated like royalty in Frau Goebblesmann's home. Wonderful breakfasts, dinners (the main meal at 1:00 p.m.), and suppers, whenever that time came around. She served us in her formal dining room. On the walls were paintings of countryside scenes. The table was set with a white cloth and a second white cloth in the center. Fresh roses from her garden, along with two candlesticks adorned the table .

The menu makes my mouth water in remembering. Breakfast featured hard-boiled eggs in small egg cups, delivered to the table in a cloth covered basket. A plate of cheese and meats, a sort of cream cheese, juice, rolls, and dark breads, jelly or jam, butter, and tea or coffee, as one preferred, accompanied the eggs.

For dinner, we enjoyed a culinary variety, including casseroles, meats, potatoes (usually in a boiled form), and salads. Nearly always we enjoyed dessert.

For supper we discovered the usual German breads, meats, and cheeses, along with surprises, and optional tea or coffee.

Always there was wine, good tasting and inexpensive, served if desired at noon, pressed upon us at supper, and simply a part of the conversation in the evening.

On a Sunday afternoon, Frau Marianne took us to the Altenburg Cathedral for a marvelous organ/choral concert. Then we walked to a classy nearby restaurant where we enjoyed waffles topped with strawberries and whipped cream. Later we visited a church-sponsored adult education academy where the director and spouse talked of their involvement in peace concerns and fed us a wonderfully spiced Hungarian goulash.

One other anecdote from Hasslinghaussen deserves mention. One morning we visited the cemetery. Yes, the cemetery. With Pastor Hafer and Frau Marianne we arrived. The cemetery occupied a promontory in the town. Individual or family grave sites lay about, defined by concrete abutments. Within the confines of each side-by-side grave site grew flowers galore of a wide variety. The families kept the sites attractive or paid to have the gardeners do it.

We walked around the cemetery and then arrived at a well-appointed chapel. We descended to the crypt below the chapel where we found, in a small workroom, the gardener and his assistant. These overalled, rough-hewn, somewhat older men smiled cordially at us and bade us sit down. Light conversation in German ensued.

It happened then that the gardener solemnly pulled a bottle out of a closet and ceremoniously unwrapped six shot glasses. He then poured vintage 1971 wine for each of us. He noted that the same vintner provided the Holy Communion wine for the churches in the area. We drank to each other's health. It was a warm human moment in the midst of death. A sort of communion in the crypt. The time: 10:00 a.m.

### An Installation in Hoyerswerda

We arrived in Hoyerswerda from Görlitz in time for the 3:30 p.m. Service of Installation for Herr Vogel as Superintendent. A fine church building in the old town provided the setting. The clergy, some twenty in number, strode in, dressed in black robes and hats, wearing white collar tabs. The organ and brass choir swelled as the clergy found their reserved front row seats. Then the service proceeded.

The East German government prided itself on allowing somewhat of a free rein to the churches. In this sense, they operated with a less restrictive policy than neighboring Soviet bloc countries such as Czechoslovakia or Poland prior to the Solidarity Movement. So, at the pastoral installation service in Hoyerswerda one could see two Communist Party officials in attendance. They sat side by side in a prominent pew, dressed in black, arms folded, faces expressionless, during the whole of the service. Both their presence and demeanor illustrated the real but strained relationship between church and state.

Following the installation in the packed church, with people of all ages, we attended the coffee hour in the fellowship hall. This, too, was something of a formal occasion. Herr Vogel proved to be a real funster. One of the clergy read a poem about Vogel written for the occasion, which brought peals of laughter from all assembled. Mary Hayworth, my colleague, remembers that Herr Fictner, our guide, translated a note in the speech of the Marxist official as, "Thanks for your kind hostility," which brought guffaws from the English speakers present. Ironic indeed!

It needs to be understood that the DDR had a constitution guaranteeing freedom of religion. This was not fully granted, but since the church through its percentage of the tax carried on the major aspects of social service, the Communist Party at times acted respectfully toward the church. So, the next speaker at the coffee hour was the female Bürgermeister, the regional Party director, who gave cordial greetings and spoke of good church–state relations.

During this latter speech, I noted the averted and pained expression on the face of Frau Vogel. The Bürgermeister said how much the government appreciated the work of the Martin Luther King House, but later we learned the extent of the struggle the strained relationship involved.

While in Hoyerswerda, Mary and I stayed with a family by the name of Brinkmann. Peter, the father, was a researcher in a laboratory, while Gersala, the mother, worked in the radiology department of a hospital. They were parents of two married daughters, one of whom attended graduate school in theology.

The Brinkmann daughter, Ulricka, age 17, still lived at home. Very bright, she had her eyes on university. To facilitate those plans she had not made her confirmation and had participated in *Jugendweihe*, the Marxist propaganda course outlined for every young person. Conversation with Ulricka showed me she shared her parents' negative attitude toward the atheistic government and its policies. Her parents preferred she refuse to take *Jugendweihe*, but with her parents support she enrolled in order more certainly to open up her future.

Some students refused *Jugendweihe*, while others took that propaganda training and confirmation. This tension-filled decision faced all young people of faith in the DDR. Refusal to take *Jugendweihe* might well adversely affect one's future, e.g., exclusion from university even though academically proficient.

## On a Rainy Saturday Morning

The second two weeks of our adventure were spent on the other side of the wall, in the DDR. Mary Hayworth and I visited Berlin, where, when moving from an Allied sector to the Soviet occupied area, we needed to stop to switch guards and crews. (The same had occurred when we crossed from the FRG to the DDR.) Mary and I walked to the wall and took pictures.

With Rev. Fictner we then began a three-hour train trip to Görlitz, passing through Lübben, Lübbenau, Cottbus, Spremberg, Harka, and other smaller villages. Görlitz lies on the Neisse River near Poland. The landscape proved flat and boring but the train ran well and on time.

Certainly the most memorable event in Görlitz took place when Cornelia, the pastor's daughter, led us on a walking tour along the streets of the city on a gray, rainy Saturday morning. We came upon a brick and concrete building, bricked up at the windows, and in obvious need of repair. Cornelia explained to us that this was the derelict synagogue of Görlitz, now abandoned and decaying. She told us only one Jew now lived in the city, married to a Hungarian now old. In the yard of this structure, with rakes, shovels, picks, and wheelbarrows at hand, we observed seven young men and women, perhaps in their twenties. The young people at work in the yard identified themselves as members of Action Reconciliation. These Christians worked in the yard to maintain the property.

We shook hands all around. The leader of the group, Ernst Oppitz, said, "We do this because we have a sense of responsibility for what happened in our country."

The group wished to repair the roof and restore the interior of the building. For whom? Why? The answers were not forthcoming. We shook hands again and walked on in the rain.

This encounter, for myself, remains the most significant moment in the totality of the German venture.

## In the Lion's Den

On our penultimate day of the German venture we visited the State Secretary's Office for Church Affairs of the DDR. The offices were formal, beautiful, and finely furnished. We sat around large tables. The welcome seemed genuine.

The official spokesperson began: In the 1950s this office for church affairs came into being. Significant growth since then. We exist to explain state policy to the churches and to see that the rights of the church are respected. New churches and redevelopment of old ones occur. On the basis of past history, the state owns some churches, but we wish we did not. We are a state institution. We know the church has a part in national life. We do not offer the church special privileges but we do protect their rights.

The official continued to speak: We do not seek to extend our atheism into the church. Rather we are here to build confidence between church and state. When problems arise we seek by dialogue to solve them. Both church and state have common interest in such dialogue. We asked about the process for dialogue. The official replied that such conversation usually began locally or at the district level. Eventually some unresolved matters may reach the head office. The conversations have included human rights, ecology, and a variety of other matters.

We asked the officials if they liked their work. They replied that if dialogue produces better understanding and reduces prejudice then they are content with their work. They went on to say, in an editorial fashion, that after the time of Martin Luther the Protestant churches were closely bound to the state. This continued through the time of the Weimar Republic, except for the Confessing Church. They opined that the church was against the working–class people. Then came, as they put it, the common struggle of some Christians with Marxists against Fascism. But many old problems still exist. But when we find common positions between church and state we enjoy it. So the officials said.

We asked if it were the task of the office to decide what theological books may be read. They responded readily, "Yes, it is our job, but most requests are granted." Here one aspect of restriction on the church shone through.

We asked how they saw the future. They said they were optimistic. They thought the World Council of Churches and the German church to be moving together in a positive direction. They said that peace and environment were on the front burner for conversation. Issues that divide appear smaller than what brings us together. Since the churches of the DDR are interested in social development, even though our foundations differ, we can and do work together.

When asked for an example of this cooperation between church and state, the officials put it this way: In the past some wanted individual rights and some social rights. Marxists see both go together. Now we sense that the churches see it that way too. So there is a consensus that "human rights cannot be used as mere propaganda."

We then expressed the sense in the churches that Christians were discriminated against on entrance to higher education. They replied in detail as follows: All have the same rights to education. We seek to implement this law, but we have more who have academic credentials than our resources and space can accommodate. Sometimes the Christian is denied entrance to university and sometimes the party member's son or daughter. If we find discrimination on religious grounds, we seek to reverse the situation. You should know that in the University of Berlin about 30–40 percent of students are Christian and in the music school it's 70–80 percent. We can show you statistics that more children of pastors find their way into university than the percentage of pastors in the population, "but we don't publicize this." It's sad that some may be left out, but "this is the way it is."

To what extent we fell subject to propaganda on this visit, who can say. The DDR government used "alternative facts" all the time. Of environmental concern, "brown coal," continued to be strip mined. You could taste the air. Many must have died of lung cancer but the government press kept extolling the cleaner air. It was a matter of grim humor in much of the population.

It was 1985. The wall was four years away from coming down. Not so much from President Reagan standing up in Berlin and shouting. No. It had mostly to do with ferment in the population and the failure of the system. People were showing up at pastor's doors and asking, "What's this

Christian stuff all about?" People were gathering in churches in large numbers and talking about politics. The pastors were telling us, "There's ferment in the air."

When Mary Hayworth and I met with church groups in the DDR we talked of peace and freedom. Vividly do I recall in the midst of such conversation a man of about thirty years stood up. "I want to say something," he said. I saw his wife reach up and pull on his pocket. He pushed her hand away. "No, I'm going to speak," he said. There was always the fear that someone in the church group had been planted by the party. If criticisms reached headquarters then there might be repercussions at the job site. More and more people took these risks.

Meanwhile Russian troops might be seen everywhere. The population loathed their presence. (Since WWII there was no love lost between Russian and German.) I walked up to a Russian officer on a town square and gave him a paper crane made by folk in our home church. (We had given these out wherever we went, made as a gift and message in our home churches.) I told him the story of the little Japanese girl, Sadako, who died of atomic bomb caused leukemia before she could make 1,000 cranes. He knew the story. He was not hostile.

## Welcoming Strangers

April 6, 1983: The newsletter for UCUP, Tacoma, Washington, contains a headline, "Invitation to Help in Refugee Resettlement." The article indicates David Bowman has agreed to sponsor a Cambodian family under the auspices of Church World Service.

April 18, 1983: Fourteen families have "volunteered to be helpers in the resettlement of the Taing family—a Kampuchean (Cambodian) family of seven." A call goes out for furnishings, clothes, etc. Tutors in English will be needed.

December 8, 1983: Twenty-five families have now volunteered to help the settlement of the Taing family, who will "arrive in a new country tomorrow with one satchel each, the clothes on their backs, $120 in cash, and hope." And then the additional welcome note: "The Church Board has given the green light to church support of this sponsorship by David Bowman."

January 25, 1984: Delayed arrival! An apartment had been rented. Damage deposit placed down. United Brokers, the leasing company, refuses to return deposit for the property on 9th Street in Tacoma. At least they will not pursue income for the six-month lease. We will anticipate arrival in April. Many belongings have arrived. More furniture needed.

March 23, 1984: The Taing family arrives. Seven in all. My wife, Dianne, and I well remember to this day the wide-eyed faces as the parents and children emerged from the customs gates at Seattle-Tacoma Airport. They are You Tea, age 30, Kim Hong, age 28, Kim Houy, age 8, Kim Cho, age 4, Soug Tech, age 2 1/2, Sun Kim, age 1 1/2, and a baby in Kim Hong's arms, Sun Eir, one month.

The newsletter then adds this sobering note: "You Tea's eldest brother, his spouse, and two children lost their lives during the tragedy of the Pol Pot regime."

April 15, 1987: The newsletter reads as follows—"Taing family quite self-sufficient." We remember with appreciation the cardinal virtues of this family: intense support of each other, sharing of resources within the family, willingness to work hard, and enthusiastic friendliness. A fine addition to this society.

For years, in addition to regular work, the family were custodians of the church. Dianne and I remain in touch with the family to this day. Kim Houy, the oldest of the seven children, has shared with us the good news, that through contact with a welcoming Christian community she became a believer. She is employed as a dental hygienist with a dentist who is a practicing Christian.

### Wheat: So Others Can Eat

Begun in 1975, the Washington Wheat Campaign proved a significant ecumenical ministry through to the time I moved to Iowa in 1988, and could no longer participate.

Operated under the aegis of the WAC, the operational concept proved successful. Those in agricultural areas of the state, especially east of the Cascade Mountains, agreed to donate grain, while church folk in urban areas donated funds to pay for the shipments abroad and to food banks across the state.

Significant to the plan, the grain shipped abroad departed Portland or Seattle to be received under the supervision of Church World Service (CWS). Always indigenous churches in the chosen recipient areas provided on-the-spot distributions. This meant no grain sat in rail cars or trucks to rot and go to waste. If local church agencies could not manage the distribution, the wheat flour went to alternate locations.

Examples of distribution are as follows: In 1976 and 1977, 500,000 pounds of wheat flour arrived in northeast Brazil. In 1978, two 100,000 pound shipments of wheat flour arrived in South Korea and the Philippines. Other shipments went to Honduras and India. In 1979, South Korea received 100,000 pounds of soybeans as "food-for-work" wages, and flood ravaged Sudan received 300,000 pounds of beans, split peas, and rice. In 1980, the donated amount of $60,000 provided seed corn for Indonesian East Timor and aided people in Niger.

Our church newsletter for UCUP, Tacoma, Washington, in April 1984, read as follows:

> The wheat shipped from Washington State, through the efforts of the Washington Wheat Campaign and CWS/CROP, arrived in Bolivia at the end of January. The Methodist Church in Bolivia reports that all but forty-one of the 3,936 bags (200,000 lb.) of wheat, which traveled by ocean freight to Peru and then overland to Bolivia, arrived in good condition. (Church leaders have made a claim for the missing bags.)

During the eleven-year ministry in Pullman, Washington, and six-year sojourn in Tacoma, Washington, I annually took a leadership role in pulling together the Spring CROP Walk, in which persons from area churches agreed to walk the miles of a designated route and giving the dollars per mile they had solicited to CWS, through the state-wide auspices of the Washington Wheat Campaign.

In the summer of 1988, we moved across country to Grinnell, Iowa, to begin a ministry there. I clearly remember that, having completed the morning service and lunch, I showed up at the Presbyterian Church to participate in the CROP Walk, picking up where I had left off in Washington.

Over the years in Washington I worked closely with Carla Vendeland, a volunteer extraordinaire, in holding educational events around the state to promote and undergird the Washington Wheat Campaign. In many ways, this developed as my primary mode of ministry beyond the local church during those years.

I wish to pay special tribute to Carla Vendeland. On behalf of the Washington Wheat Campaign, she was a whirling dervish. At one point, she traveled to Brazil to inspect how efficiently the grain arrived at its destination. Her enthusiasm for hunger response spilled over on many people, including me.

Cancer took Carla in 1994 at age 52. At her service Rev. Loren Arnett, retired Executive Minister of the WAC, said "She saw her work fighting hunger as the way she acted out her own faith . . . I think she worked too hard. But she was driven."

One of the saints along the way.

# That They May All Be One

Grant, O Lord, that thy church, as it hath one foundation and one head, may truly be one body, holding one faith, proclaiming one truth, and following one Lord in holiness of living and love, even thy Son our Savior, Jesus Christ. Amen.

Howard Paine & Bard Thompson, *Book of Prayers for Church and Home*[1]

---

1. Paine and Thompson, *Book of Prayers*, 46.

## A Shared Vision

DURING THE THREE YEARS of ministry at Park Church, Grand Rapids, Michigan, I enjoyed comradeship with Rev. David Killian, a Paulist priest, who along with three other teachers operated the Catholic Information Center in downtown Grand Rapids. Together we played some golf and ate spicy spaghetti, prepared by my wife, Dianne, at our home in Comstock Park.

We shared a significant adult education ministry in the downtown. In the spring of 1969, 1970, and 1971 we conducted an adult film series on Wednesday noons at the Information Center and Wednesday evenings at Park Church. Our audience for the noon hour showings depended largely on those who would spill out of their offices. We provided for them coffee and sandwiches. Our evening viewers came predominantly from the Park Church congregation. We ran six renewals of this service in six to eight week segments over the three-year span. They were well attended.

The format was simple indeed. We projected creative short fictional story films containing implied gems of meaning. These films averaged twelve minutes in length. We then opened the floor for lively discussion of the meanings and applications for our lives based on what we had viewed together.

These brief visuals were similar to what might be seen on the PBS program, "Independent Lens." Such films as "The Chicken," "Little Blue, Little Yellow," "Rhinoceros," "The Hangman," "Alf, Bill and Fred," and many others appeared. In one advance notice we announced, "The eight films explore human relationships, the mystery of life, art and creativity, war and the psychology of violence, ecology, racism, and the human future." Quite a menagerie.

Writing of these episodes decades later, I remember only one of these films in any detail: "It's About This Carpenter." This 1963 film, directed by Lewis Teague and produced by New York University's Department of Television, purports to be "recreation in modern terms of Christ's last journey." We see a carpenter creating a sizeable wooden cross, much to the annoyance of his wife, in his Greenwich Village apartment. He exits the apartment, straps the cross to the back of his motor scooter and heads out, only to be stopped by a policeman. He parks his vehicle and enters the subway bearing the cross. It's crowded. Passengers eye him as if he's their chief villain. Exiting the subway to the street, a small girl leans over the rail and says with a smile, "Hello, Jesus!"

He hurries on. On foot. He arrives at the church. No one greets or welcomes him. Only the organist at practice notices him and waves him away. He finds the appointed place and attaches the cross to the wall. The church now houses the cross, though without welcoming it or its bearer. The carpenter, his journey finished, retraces his steps. Descending the subway steps, the little girl once again greets him. "Hello, Jesus!"

The journey of the carpenter is ended. At every stage he's been abused and rejected. Only the little girl at the subway stairs knows who he is—and welcomes him. "Out of the mouths of babes!" One is reminded of the crucifixion scene in St. Mark's Gospel where only the centurion knows who he is, "Truly this man was God's Son" (15:39).

As I look back on a ministry full of emphasis on adult education, this series stands out. Ecumenical! Animated! Insightful! It's about this vision.

Since those days, Rev. Killian left the Paulist Order, became an Episcopal rector, married Barbara, adopted two wonderful Korean children (Brendon and Meeya), and carried on a creative ministry in an Episcopal parish on Beacon Street in Boston. We have stayed in touch.

## The Spirit Is A Moverin'

On Sunday, May 30, 1971, an ecumenical gathering convened on Calder Plaza in the heart of Grand Rapids, Michigan. The occasion? Pentecost Sunday.

A "stabile," dark red in color, stands prominently on a concrete plaza in mid-city Grand Rapids. This abstract metal sculpture came from the creative hand of the American artist, Alexander Calder (1898–1976). Around this impressive piece titled, "Le Grande Vitisse," ("grand swiftness" or "grand rapids"), the event took place.

What an impressive centerpiece! Standing forty-three feet tall, fifty-four feet long, thirty feet wide, and weighing in at forty-two tons. Calder, noted for his "mobiles," which were in motion, spoke of these as "stabiles," which were designed, as Wikipedia puts it, "to activate a viewer's motion." Thus, the sculpture's meaning coincides with the meaning of the first Christian Pentecost, the movement of the divine Spirit activating and putting into motion the first followers of Jesus Christ. That symbolic sense did not come to mind in 1971, but it was just the right place to gather.

I remember concocting this celebration with Rev. Killian. In those conversations he persuaded me that inclusion of the Jewish community, the original keepers of Pentecost, would enhance the celebration.

Lots of people participated. Banners were carried by seven groups. Park Church provided liturgical dance and New Hope Baptist brought the choir. Rabbi Joel Chazen led a rite of penitence and hope. At the close of the service we shared matzo (unleavened bread), the "bread of freedom," commemorative of the Hebrew Exodus and representing the continuing meaning of liberation in our world.

I possess in my file a copy of the service, noteworthy by the abstract design for Pentecost. The abstract design denoting wind and fire on bright green paper, including around the margins a prayer, "Come, Holy Spirit, rekindle in us the fire of your love . . . " and the Hebrew greeting, "Shalom." A member of Park Church, Ilse Eerdmans, a part of the famous Eerdmans Publishing family, rendered that artistic cover.

In the aftermath of the event, attended by hundreds, a letter arrived from Russell H. McConnell, Executive Director, Grand Rapids Area Council of Churches, reading in part, "The Calder Plaza service was effective and very much worthwhile." He called it "a significant ecumenical witness."

## The Clergy Group

Wherever I engaged in parish ministry I participated actively in the clergy group of that area. Such gatherings, usually monthly, often move about from church to church. As a United Church of Christ clergyman with "united" in the name, active interchurch involvement is, in part, the name of the game.

Upon landing in Pullman, Washington, I recall a conservative Baptist pastor, to my surprise, invited me to coffee and to the clergy gathering. I found special collegial relationship with the United Methodist minister, Rev. William Berney, leading to our churches sharing summer services and musical events.

The more conservative Protestant clergy did not connect with the groupings. I recall however, that the Missouri Synod Lutheran Church pastor shared regularly in the group, though in other locations "Missouri" has not usually been present. I recall an incident at a clergy meeting in Angola, Indiana. Two Missouri Synod Lutherans usually attended. Another attendee, a Lutheran pastor, serving an Evangelical Lutheran Church in America congregation, had formerly served a Missouri church in Fort Wayne. After a meeting he walked up to the two Missouri men (always men) and asked, "If I showed up in one of your churches, would you commune me?" Without hesitation, they responded, "No." So much for "that they may be one."

Catholic priests in some locations were involved. I do recall this to be true of Rev. Charles Skok, of Sacred Heart parish in Pullman. Then a reversal. A letter came from the Vatican through the Spokane bishop's office to him saying that this extensive fraternization with Protestants must end. He had been in my pulpit and I in his. Vividly do I recall Skok's newsletter in which he said though withdrawal from such ecumenical involvement pained him deeply, as a loyal son of the church, he must obey. Pope John Paul II, the "Polish pope," one of the giants of the twentieth century, possessed many graces. An ecumenical vision was not one of them.

Sometimes the clergy groups included persons not in our usual mainstream. In a couple of cases, Seventh Day Adventists participated. In other cases, we were pleased to associate with a representative of the Reorganized Church of Latter Day Saints (RLDS), headquartered in Independence Missouri, not Salt Lake, Utah. When we planned a shared worship, including our RLDS member, a couple of our clergy members found themselves stretched beyond their ecumenical limits.

In large measure, over the years, our clergy group meetings were not something worth writing home about. Normally we would announce anything in our own bailiwicks of more general interest. In one place we one by one shared our own "spiritual journey." In several places we developed unified Good Friday services and, in a couple of places, met together to observe in January the Week of Prayer for Christian Unity. In several places, we jointly sponsored the CWS CROP Walk for Hunger. Often we shared

Thanksgiving services. At Bethel Church, in Manchester, Michigan, we kept both Ash Wednesday and Good Friday services together.

In my last parish setting, Faith Lutheran of Los Gatos, California, the clergy group expressed broader diversity. Year after year, led by Rabbi Melody Aron of Congregation–Shir Hadash, the group contained Unitarian–Universalists, the Center for Spiritual Enlightenment, Muslims, Church of Christ Scientists, and sometimes others. We sponsored well-attended Thanksgiving services. This diversity I found of value, though efforts to carry out ecumenical Christian worship or other endeavors were hampered. I pulled together one poorly attended Good Friday service.

Always I have felt both the potential of such clergy groups and the lack of fulfillment. Organized, and with focused agenda, these groups could make an immense difference. Why does this not happen? Easy. Most clergy are heavily involved in their own parish; the ecumenical work receives short shrift. Plus, ecumenism is hard work, since often one is eking out new territory where few precedents prevail. Oh, and one more obstacle: Clergy are often a bit chary of providing venues where laity will see firsthand what's going on elsewhere. That parish member might find the grass greener across the fence.

An example of the clergy working together in a new and creative way took place while I served Bethel Church. Under the planning of the Ministerial Association, and at my instigation, we invited Rev. Bert Marshall, a UCC pastor, to come among us for a special event. He came with something special on his mind, namely the Gospel According to St. Mark. As he had done before in numerous locations, in dramatic fashion he delivered the gospel from memory to a large and enthralled ecumenical congregation. It was indeed a memorable occasion to hear the evangel presented, not in piece-meal fashion, but the whole of the sixteen chapters from "The beginning of the good news of Jesus Christ . . . " to " . . . and they[the women] said nothing to anyone for they were afraid" (Mark 1:1 and 16:18).

## Keeping a Midweek Appointment

We met each Wednesday morning. About ten of us. Ecumenical, we were. Mostly liberal Protestants and a couple of Catholics. Clergy types seeking to run through the brambles of the parish while keeping personal lives on track.

Each Wednesday, unless professional or personal emergencies interfered, we gathered. Young, we occupied roles in parish life subordinate to older professionals. The tensions within those relationships constituted a good deal of the conversation.

It was the era of sensitivity training. Feelings, not concepts, lay in ascendancy. "How do you feel about this or that?" seemed the key question.

Rev. Alland, a counseling minister of Disciples of Christ background, who along with his spouse, Rosemary, had spent time in what was then known as The Congo (now Central African Republic), convened the meetings. The procedure then took on the aspect of ritual. We moved around the room verbally checking as to where we were in mind and spirit. Then some sort of consensus developed as to which of the fellows required the "help seat" for the day, if he wanted to occupy that spot. Then the conversation proceeded with focus on that person.

We could have engaged in some other exchange. A shared study of the lectionary, for example. Or we might have exchanged ideas about proper strategies for parish life. But that was not the era. Self-examination in support groups—that agenda rose to the fore.

For me, in general, it proved useful. I grew in genuine care for those guys. Though learning to be a pastor, where care for others is tantamount, protection of myself lay close to my heart. Raised to experience "perfect love," my own priorities, in fact, pointed elsewhere. This Wednesday group provided an incubator where real feelings of care grew and matured.

I say more. Over a couple of years, I came to believe the process of the group saved a couple of guys for the ministry, maybe even spared a couple of lives. The inner life of the parish is strewn with landmines born of complex relationships with staff and parishioners. Finding those with skill and caring who could provide sounding boards made a lot of difference—positive difference. The capacity to love others grew significantly for me through that group.

There's a negative side. *C'est la vie!* In the third year a fellow revealed that he and his spouse and another couple were experimenting with the limits of their relationships—together. He found himself wanting to check out the reactions of the group. From my point of view several in the group were far too accepting of this adventure in intimacy. I spoke up—it seemed against the stream—to the effect that life itself offered enough trials for married life without tempting fate. I sensed that my point of view ran counter to the consensus in the group. After that I began to find other things to do on Wednesday mornings.

I think it correct to say that growing out of the intimacy experiment, one marriage fell apart and the other barely survived.

Since we were committed to confidentiality in the group, even to share the above strains the edges of the fabric. Maybe it's long enough ago that the statute of limitations came and went.

## United Ministries: A Unique Regional Ecumenical Experiment

At the same time my family and I arrived in Pullman, Washington, the newborn United Ministries (UM) emerged on the other side of the Cascade Mountains. For the next 14 years, until its demise in the fall of 1985, I played an active role in its joys and sorrows.

Rev. Jim Halfaker, the UCC Conference Minister for the Washington-North Idaho Conference, tells me that the idea came from the ecumenist, Rev. David Colwell, while pastoring at Plymouth Congregational UCC in Seattle. He convinced Rev. Jim Smucker of the new possibilities, just prior to Smucker's going to New York as Conference Minister.

United Ministries had a Trinitarian shape—about one hundred UCC churches, about eighty Disciples congregations, and about ten Brethren congregations.

United Ministries went through three organizational configurations. At the outset all denominational staff retained their denominational employment. The second covenant, begun in 1974, involved professional staff, except for the conference (UCC) and regional (Disciples) ministers, employed under the UM umbrella. At that point Rev. Frank Kelsey became the Executive Minister for UM, a post he held until 1985. Summer 1979 saw the emergence of a more denominational, less UM oriented organizational shape.

During the course of UM, members of the Pullman Congregational Church played an active role. For a time, I served as chair of the UCC Board of Directors and on the UM Executive Committee. Monica Peters served in various decision-making roles over a considerable period of time. In 1978, Don Peters presented to the UM assembly a resolution from our church opposing the death penalty. Others, including Bob and Sally Floren, Carl Stevens, Sue Schell, Marj Grunewald, and Irene McAllister, were involved.

Various virtues shown through the fabric of the UM structure. People appreciated the large annual worship and fellowship occasions. The social activism of the UCC contributed to the Disciples and Brethren. The peace witness of the Brethren, while not particularly strong in the region, lent a positive influence.

On the other hand, problems dogged the UM from the outset. I remember the consternation in UCC circles when it emerged that the Disciples' contingent could not guarantee an annual dollar amount for the UM budget, since the money flowed to Indianapolis, the Disciples' headquarters, before a portion of it came back to Seattle. This pattern made it difficult for the Disciples to guarantee a certain amount to the budget. Jim Halfaker believes the failure of the Disciples and Brethren to meet budget deadlines played a critical role in the demise of UM.

In the final analysis, or "the bottom line" as they say, perhaps Bob Floren said it best: "The task of uniting three denominations is immense and I'm not sure it will ever be realized." Jim Halfaker reports that other denominational leaders in the area were "puzzled" by the UM arrangement. He adds that the denominational leaders in headquarters never paid much attention to the experiment in ecumenicity.

My own astonishment lies in the lack of collected historical record extant describing the course of United Ministries. The UCC records lie scattered in the archives of the Washington Historical Society. Given the hue and cry for church mergers in the late 20th century, one would think there ought to exist a careful analysis and clear record of what went right and what went wrong. This vacuum reminds me of the Roman Catholic novelist, J. F. Powers, who in fiction such as *Morte D'Urban* and *Wheat That Springeth Green*, affectionately, but sadly, describes the bumbling nature of the ecclesiastical process. People say they object to "the organized church" but just when did they ever see the church really organized?

For a time, I flew from Pullman to Seattle on Cascade Airlines, the twelve-seat puddle jumper. On one occasion, flying into Spokane, the midrange stop en route across the Cascades, we swooped into the airport, only to zoom up sharply. Through the curtain, the pilot said, "I didn't think we were going to make it that time, so I thought we'd go back up and try again." Thereafter, I drove to Spokane and boarded the "yellow banana" of Hughes Airwest. Passengers were served international cheeses, a variety of crackers, a piece of fruit, and a small bottle of Spanish or French wine. Excellent! A real sacrifice on behalf of UM.

I spent much time flying back and forth to meetings in Seattle, and plying I-5 after we moved to Tacoma, all seeking to be a valuable cog in the UM machine. I think, on the whole, my time was well spent. I do recall, however, that at one point in a UCC board meeting in 1985, I raised my hand and moved that the UCC remove its support for the continuation of UM. Of the dissolution, Jim Halfaker reports, "I had personally to take that word to the Disciples and Brethren, who were in different rooms. It was a heavy day."

So, a lament for old UM. An ecumenical child withering and dying in its adolescence. Who knows, maybe the main problem was cultural. Someone once noted that after a joint meeting the UCC folk gathered at the bar, the Disciples assembled at the ice cream parlor, and the Brethren hurried home to sleep.

Jesus prayed, "That they may be one . . . " (John 17:21), so St. John tells us. But what really did Jesus mean? Organizational unity? If so, we reply, "But, Lord, it's so hard to achieve."

## A Visit to the Synagogue

I always took my confirmation class participants, as part of the curriculum, to a Jewish Synagogue and an Eastern Orthodox Church.

In 1984, while at UCUP, Tacoma, Washington, we set out on a Sunday afternoon to the nearby Conservative/Reform Synagogue, this time for a tour rather than a service. We had made an appointment with Rabbi Rosenthal to show us around. Much to our disappointment, on arrival, the secretary informed us that the rabbi suddenly had been called away at the death of a one-hundred-year-old member of the congregation. In his place, a *bar mitzvah* young man, named Joseph, about fifteen years of age.

That particular synagogue, Temple Beth El, features much symbolism. Poignant remembrances of the Holocaust include a child's drawing embedded in the architecture. As Joseph showed us around it became clear he possessed encyclopedic sort of knowledge of the scene. When I arrived home I said to my wife, Dianne, "The rabbi was called away. A young man conducted the tour. We didn't miss the rabbi at all."

Later on, Joseph Kanofsky became well known to us as a school friend of our daughters. He attended Boston University where, as a student, he was a reader for the famed writer and Holocaust survivor, Elie Wiesel. He studied with Professor Wiesel from 1987 to 1998.

Joseph's parents practiced the Jewish faith in a modest manner, parallel to those Christians who show up at church on Christmas and Easter. Early on Joseph began to display deeper diligence. Following his schooling he served as Rabbi in Warsaw, Poland, the scene of disaster for Jews leading to and during World War II. Currently Rabbi Yossel is Rabbi at Kehillat Sharei Torah, an Orthodox synagogue in the suburbs of Toronto, Canada. He and his spouse, Sharona, are parents of six children, Avraham, Moshe, Mendy, Jaakov, Shalom, and Shaira.

It happened in Boston that when Sharona had delivered their first child, Avraham, I was privileged to visit their hospital room. A Gentile paying Avraham a visit! Joseph and Sharona welcomed me and shared the joy of the occasion. Then gently Joseph indicated that a special custom must occur at sunset. They would need to be alone. I left feeling that once again Joseph had conducted the tour well, this time in concert with Sharona. (Back from two years of study in Israel, Avraham is now a student at the University of Toronto in computer science and philosophy.)

We stay in touch. A couple of years ago Joseph corresponded with me remembering the large sign board standing at a busy intersection on the corner of our church property. Joseph remembered that instead of worship times, and other announcements, I posted, week by week, thought provoking epigrams. Joseph indicated he now had a similar sign board on the synagogue property and could I remember any of my pithy pronouncements? I sent him my favorite, "Eschew obfuscation." He sent back his approval. Gentile passersby might think it's some ancient Hebrew pronouncement.

Did I send Joseph another of my favorites? I'm not sure. It's perhaps more current now as the author is none other than the 2016 Nobel Prize Winner for Literature, Bob Dylan. The sign read, "You gotta serve somebody . . . Bob Dylan."

It so happens that tall and dense brush stood below the above-mentioned church sign. I remember looking out my office window to see a police vehicle pulled in under that bushy camouflage waiting for some unsuspecting driver to run the stop sign. I grabbed my camera and shot the scene. Indeed, as Robert Allen Zimmerman (b.1941), of Duluth, Minnesota, once said, "You gotta serve somebody."

## A New Theological Child is Born

During my years in University Place, Tacoma, Washington, a fledgling theological seminary opened in Seattle. The Northwest Theological Union (NTU) located itself in free office and classroom space provided in Campion Tower at Seattle University. Beginning on October 1, 1984, by May 11, 1985, seventy-five students had enrolled in classes. Its broad ecumenical base included incorporating committee members Rev. Rodney Romney of First Baptist Church and Rabbi Earl Starr of Temple De Hirsch Sinai.

Rev. J. Lynwood Walker, a man with a joint PhD from University of California at Berkeley and the Graduate Theological Union, founded NTU, along with his spouse, Ginger, who directed development and public relations. Nothing of this nature was available in the Pacific Northwest.

During terms in 1986 and 1987 I taught three courses at NTU—Introduction to Christian Ethics, A Biblical Life Ethic: Abortion, Capital Punishment, and War, and The Writings of C.S. Lewis.

Lyn Walker and Robert Schmidt, chair of Academic Offices, began to project a fund-raising campaign of five million dollars with purposes of setting up divisions of NTU in Oregon, Central and Eastern Washington, Idaho, and Alaska. Big plans indeed.

After involvement in NTU for a while, I thought all was moving along normally. Then I began to wonder about the financial status of the project. Several times I inquired of the office, asking for an annual financial report. Nothing was forthcoming. So, I stopped by one afternoon asking Lyn Walker for a copy of such a report. Immediately he became hostile and showed me the door. I left and never went back. As I left I had a sense that something did not smell good at NTU.

Rev. James Halfaker, former Conference Minister, Washington/N. Idaho Conference, UCC, informs me that NTU was not able to achieve accreditation through the American Association of Theological Schools. Without much communication among supporting people, the Walkers closed the doors and moved to Georgia, "leaving lots of pain." By 1991 NTU was no more.

The Walkers did have a creative idea. With the leadership of Rev. William Sullivan, President of Seattle University, an ecumenical group picked up the pieces. James Halfaker, fresh from several years of fund raising for the UCC nationally, agreed to raise funds for a new entity, the Institute of Ecumenical Theological Studies. The pieces came together.

Today, while theological schools flounder here and there, a lively School of Theology and Ministry (STM) thrives in Seattle, incorporating Catholics and a variety of Protestant participants, including African Methodist Episcopal, American Baptist, Christian (Disciples of Christ), Church of the Brethren, Community of Christ, Lutheran ELCA, Presbyterian(USA), United Church of Christ, and United Methodist. As of Spring 2017, eighty Protestant students were enrolled at STM.

Out of the ashes. Thanks be to God.

## A Sparkling Ecumenicity

During my six-year stint at the church in University Place, Tacoma, Washington, I invested time and energy in the ecumenical work of Associated Ministries of Pierce County. Under the leadership of Rev. David Alger, that ministry fulfilled its goal as "A crossroad to communication and cooperation witnessing to Christian unity in action." For several years, I was an active member of the board.

Usually in February, Associated Ministries sponsored Communiversity, an adult Christian education event of four weeks on Sunday afternoons. A keynote speaker kicked off the month's well-attended sessions. Some dozen or so classes drew attendees each year.

I taught at Communiversity for three years. In 1983, I taught "A Biblical Life Ethic," taking up the subjects of abortion, capital punishment, and participation in war. The next year, 1984, I announced "What Does the Future Hold?" as my course title, taking a look at biblical themes, contemporary authors as diverse as Hal Lindsey, Loren Eiseley, Walker Percy, and Frederick Buechner, and assessing the thrust of "New Age" thought on the subject. Then, in 1985, we explored in seminar fashion the biblical wisdom Book of Ecclesiastes, under the title, "Qoheleth—An Indirect Witness to Christ," noting especially the writings of Robert Short, he of *The Gospel According to Peanuts* fame.

My involvement continued right up to the close of my ministry in Tacoma. I possess a copy of a letter, dated May 11, 1988, where I, on behalf of the Communiversity subcommittee on curriculum, invited Sally Alger, spouse of David, to teach a February, 1989, course on "Christianity and the Graphic Arts." Bringing together Catholics and Protestants of a wide variety of hues, Communiversity year after year provided opportunity for Christians to learn together.

## Statewide Prayers

In 1984, while Chair of the WAC, we wrote and distributed around the state an ecumenical prayer calendar. By using the calendar Roman Catholics would pray for Baptists, Lutherans for Presbyterians, etc.

The format of the document deserves notice. Each month identified a problem, described a church response, offered a pertinent biblical text, and then presented a paragraph prayer.

The problems identified over a twelve-month period and the ministry response included the plight of the elderly in Spokane served by the ecumenical Mid–City Concerns, the struggle of persons on the Yakima Indian Reservation responded to by a Christian Church/Disciples mission, and the needs of incarcerated persons in Washington State prisons eliciting a response from Matthew House led by Rev. Richard Stohr. These are but three of the twelve presented.

Within the identity of St. Leo's Parish in the heart of Tacoma, Washington, the material described the Hospitality Kitchen and the Food Connection which served 8,000 people each month. The biblical text quoted:

> The kind of fasting I want is this: Remove the chains of oppression and the yoke of injustice, and let the oppressed go free. Share your food with the hungry and open your homes to the homeless poor. Give clothes to those who have nothing to wear . . . (Isa 58:6–7).

Then came the prayer:

> Eternal God, giver of our daily bread, we are sad because despite the bounty of our harvests, there are those who go to bed hungry. We pray that the ministry at St. Leo's may have resources to respond to the needs of all who enter its doors. Let the bread they give be the Bread of Life. Amen.

While this shared endeavor lies as a mere blip on the screen of ecclesiastical history, yet it provides a small portrait of the statewide endeavors of the ecumenical church in a more ecumenical era. The picture: Christians of a wide diversity reaching out to others and praying for each other's efforts. Surely this effort moved in the direction of Jesus' comment, according to St. John, "By this everyone will know that you are my disciples, if you have love for one another" (John 13:35).

Were we not approaching the admonition to "provide one another to long and good deeds" (Heb 10:24) and paying attention to the pastoral advice, "Let mutual love continue" (Heb 13:1)?

# Conflict and Resolution

And after Paul and Barnabas had *no small dissension and debate* with them, Paul and Barnabas and some of the others were appointed to go up to Jerusalem to discuss this question with the apostles and the elders.

Acts 15:2

## Facing the Format of Worship

Park Church, UCC, since 1846, lies in the heart of Grand Rapids, Michigan. The big pile of yellow bricks housed Congregational Christians since 1867. The building appeared at a cost of $75,000.

The sanctuary sits at a second floor level above the ground floor, reached by stairs or elevators. Carved wood depicting vines, grapes, and Christian symbols adorn the walls, the flanks of the chancel, and the chancel furniture. Through the arch over the altar the reredos presents a carved figure of Christ, accomplished by Alvis Lang, he a descendant of a long line of wood carvers of religious imagery. (One may remember that Grand Rapids features a history of wood furniture.) A fine Aeolian–Skinner pipe organ completed the scene. The piece *de resistance*—twelve large genuine Tiffany windows offering biblical scenes. A dignified center for worship indeed.

In 1970, questions arose in the congregation about the format of worship. The Board of Deacons instituted a Worship Committee to study various proposals for change. One member couple had written to the Chair of the Deacons, William Banta, proposing changes from a "too stylized" pattern. They also thought the younger clergy, Rev. Alland and myself, might preach more often. Others preferred a steady-as-she-goes arrangement.

Enter the clergy. Rev. McKenney, Senior Minister, wrote to the Deacons a three-page position paper on worship. In essence, he proposed a maintenance of the worship *status quo* as a proper stance for "one of the great churches of our city and land." Without invitation, but in my role as "minister to the whole church," I too wrote a position paper to the Board. In that paper, I asked for modest liturgical variation, more frequent practice of Holy Communion, and a search for "a greater sense of warmth" in the worship hour.

As a part of McKenney's paper, he requested that the Worship Committee be disbanded. He wrote me personally complaining that nobody had requested my advice. He barred me from further relationship to the Board and Worship Committee. The Board complied with McKenney's request.

Not long afterward, Richard Gazella resigned as Chair of the already defunct Worship Committee. He wrote "I regret the decision of Dr. McKenney of severing the relationship of Associate Minister, Rev. Bowman, from the Board of Deacons and, also, our Worship Committee." He further wrote, "It was not the committee's desire . . . to radically change our format of worship all at once. However, certain changes, small or large, could make our worship service more meaningful."

About the same time Mr. Gazella resigned, September 1970, I wrote to McKenney, saying, "Because it concerns vitally my own attempt to minister here at Park Church I once again, in all respect, ask you to consider again the issue of the frequency of my pulpit ministry." More frequent occasions were not allotted.

Once, in the midst of the ongoing tension over worship and other matters, I offered a pulpit word titled, "Christians Argue Too." The essence of these remarks simply pointed to the historical fact of disagreement among Christians over matters simple and complex, minor and important. I called for what I named, "constructive dialogue."

Rev. McKenney took that topic as too provocative. He observed to me, "I've learned never to say anything controversial in the pulpit." I did not reply. To myself I muttered, "Really?"

## Speaking Ex Cathedra

On May 7, 1969, I wrote the "From the Minister's Desk" column for the "Park Congregationalist," the weekly newsletter from Park Church in Grand Rapids, Michigan.

The brief piece contained some florid, predictive remarks, such as, "The dying gasps of narrow nationalism are heard across the land." And, "There is some reason for optimism if we can hear the call of God leading from restrictive provincialism to commitments at once more open and more intensive!"

The context of these remarks? The Vietnam conflict. Young people cried aloud, "They are our brothers whom we kill." I claimed that the onset of the "global village," brought about by new modes of mobility and communication, provided young people with a different set of perspectives and loyalties reaching beyond national borders. Noting that "Nationalism has resulted in much human carnage over the last 125 years," I expressed hope for political allegiances "less limited by boundaries of time and space."

Two days later, May 9, I received a letter from a Park Church member. It contained a cut out copy of my May 7 piece. In part, Mr. Edward Larson wrote, "It is the sort of droppings of a vain man we do not want in our house . . . Do you think you are on earth in the year 1969 to be the great light? Pure vanity . . . Consider yourself and then ask a question 'Who would really follow me across the street?'"

On May 10, 1969, I replied by letter to Mr. Larson. Regrettably, I did not retain a copy of that correspondence, nor of any reply.

Looking back on the scene forty-seven years later, I smile to myself. Maybe the concern for "narrow nationalism" and changing political perspectives merited reflection but I do sound as if it were to be signed by H.V. Kaltenborn or Eric Sevareid, rather than the Associate Minister at Park Church. Perhaps "droppings of vain man" annoying the household rings a bit harsh, but Mr. Larson may have been on to something. I was young and feeling my oats.

A term occurs to me: Pontificate. Meaning to "deliver oracular utterances or dogmatic opinions." So, thank you, Mr. Larson. You might have approached with a gentler demeanor but you participated in my clergy education. Whatever my current faults, I am less prone to utterances from on high, especially those too ready to invoke God's will.

## Welcoming Refugees with a Slap in the Face

Those were the mid-seventies. In the State of Washington, Governor Evans began welcoming Southeast Asian refugees fleeing Vietnam and Cambodia due to ravages of the war. Churches began to open their doors as sponsors of these "huddled masses, yearning to breathe free."

As pastor of a congregation in Pullman, Washington, I had decided there were too many rational reasons why we were not well prepared to be a welcoming congregation and sponsor a family. But I had not reckoned with Irene Spencer, a firm and well-intentioned member of the congregation.

Without any signal from me, she began to put the sponsoring wheels in motion. Thinking she might be right, and wanting to appear the leader I was supposed to be, I ran to catch up. In the summer of 1975 we welcomed the Dang The Coung family of eight from Cambodia.

We made arrangements with a Pullman family, not members in the congregation, to become the host family. All seemed well. All well until the father appeared at the parsonage door saying, "Mrs. So and So, the hostess, slapped my teenage daughter in the face because she didn't like the way she was doing dishes."

I was furious. The purpose of all this was not indentured servitude, with the additional burden of unwarranted abuse. This situation could not stand. As soon as possible we moved the family to a welcoming situation, much to the relief of the newcomers.

Some days later I began to descend the back stairs of the church building. Who should be ascending but Mrs. So and So. She looked me in the face, her own visage livid. "Bowman," she snarled, "you're nothing!"

I recall the first thought that sprang to my mind, "Well, she must be wrong since God don't make junk." I do not recall the remainder of the conversation, which I believe was short-lived.

Upon reflection now, perhaps there might have ensued some negotiation that would have saved the face of the host family. Perhaps. I doubt it.

In retrospect, I do not regret having acted with dispatch to relieve the situation as soon as other suitable quarters could be found.

Also on reflection, I think of what must have troubled that father's mind, saying to himself, "What sort of reception is this? A slap in the face of my beloved daughter." I remember he did not dawdle. No grass grew under his feet before he knocked on the parsonage door.

Led by parish members, Irene and Roger Spencer and Beverly and Pat McConnell, undeterred by the untoward incident, the sponsorship of refugees continued over at least a seven year period. In 1978, the Le and Luong families arrived. Later the Laird and Ellen Hastay family of our parish sponsored Pham Hung Van and Pham Thieu Chi. In 1980 the Pullman Cambodian Relief Committee formed out of strong leadership from our parish and in cooperation with Common Ministry on the WSU campus.

Parish, the Thought

## The New Age Up Close

During the years 1982 to 1988 I served the UCUP, Tacoma, Washington. Up in Yelm, Washington, near Mount Rainier, a former housewife, J. Z. Knight, claimed to channel Ramtha, "the alleged 35,000–year–old ascended master from the lost continent of Atlantis. She had enticed movie celebrities, such as Shirley MacLaine and Linda Evans, to buy homes nearby in order to be in touch with the weird program. A visit to Yelm revealed a modest rural community surrounding her walled–in mansion, with turrets and wind-swept banners visible above the walls, looking like a royal, medieval castle. The ancient Ramtha's voice included advice on strategies to purchase Ms. Knight's Arabian horses.

Closer to home, "new age" notions appeared in the pews and choir loft of our church. Professor Richard Overman, a choir member whose son, Bob, directed the choir, taught religion at nearby University of Puget Sound. He, a United Methodist minister, serving in his teaching role "beyond the local church," believed, in so many words, that the Christian faith had become lost in Egypt in the first century but that the "new age" movement was in process of rediscovering the true faith.

"New age" may be described as the warmed over perennial philosophy of Gnosticism. The Gnostics views received further elucidation in the Nag Hammadi find in Egypt in 1945. Philip J. Lee has given a succinct description of this view: " . . . alienation from the world, secret knowledge, escape from the world, escape into self and special status for the knowledgeable ones."[1]

Not long after I donned the mantle of ministry at UCUP, tensions began to rise between Professor Overman's new ageism and my own incarnational orthodoxy. As time went on I sensed myself from the pulpit interpreting the scriptural text, emphasizing themes which contradicted "new age" dogma. I reflected to myself, "Well, if we have controversy at least it's not over the color of the sanctuary carpet; rather it involves discerning the truth of the faith once delivered to the saints."

An instance of the controversy developed when the choir, of the aforementioned Bob Overman, decided to sing an arrangement of W. B. Yeats' poem, "Sailing to Byzantium." Yeats, a long–time adherent of gnostic teachings, wrote in part:

---

1. Lee, *Against the Protestant Gnostics*, 176.

## Conflict and Resolution

> O sages standing in God's holy fire
> As in the gold mosaic of a wall,
> Come from the holy fire, perne in a gyre,
> And be the singing masters of my soul.
> Consume my heart away, sick with desire
> And fastened to a dying animal
> It knows not what it is; and gather me
> Into the artifice of eternity.[2]

Here the reader discerns antagonism to incarnation (dying animal) and receives the notion of the soul's escape from the body (steal my heart away) rather than spying a picture of resurrection. I asked that this anthem not be sung in the worship hour by the choir, since its themes strove mightily against key elements of the Christian faith. I was told, "We will sing it." It was sung. So much for my pastoral authority. The dye was cast.

Another instance of "new age" appeared for me on the regional church level. The Board of the Washington–North Idaho Conference, UCC, asked another minister and myself to review the credentials and philosophy of a clergy candidate for ordination. It developed in conversation that he taught both resurrection and reincarnation doctrines simultaneously. We indicated our puzzlement about that since surely these two views were inimical to each other. He, however, remained adamant. In his mind, there existed no conflict. We took him at his word and recommended that as long as he held this view he not be considered a viable candidate.

Toward the close of ministry in Tacoma, the ideological dispute came more into the open. At a regional meeting, Professor Overman and I held a debate over the virtues and vices of "new age."

In the sixth year of my ministry in that parish, Overman invited his sycophants to his house for a rump session designed to oust me from my post. (Such meetings fell outside the by-laws of the church.) Ironically enough, he had been the main proponent of my coming to that parish. He liked the fact of my earned doctoral degree, but I did not prove malleable to his views of the faith.

I could have won a numerical battle and stayed the course. (The ouster petition listed forty-three solicited names. I quickly had eighty-seven unsolicited supportive names.) But there were other facets of incompatibility for me in that parish. I had no further stomach for a continual battle, even

---

2. Yeats, *Modern Poetry*, 77–78.

though the record shows I fiercely defended the resilience and effectiveness of my ministry there. Already I had my profile out in search of another parish in which to serve the Lord and others.

The letter to the Pastor–Parish Relations Committee, calling for my ouster, alluded to several skills in my ministry and named no defects, except to say that "certain personal and religious needs of people in our congregation" would be better served if the ministry were discontinued. The first three of the forty-three signatures were Richard, Phyllis, and Bob Overman.

In the August 1988, church newsletter I wrote, in part:

> I recall that on 17 October 1982 in the installation service I promised "to execute this charge with faithfulness, to preach and teach the word of God, to administer the sacraments, and to fulfill the pastoral office."
>
> Relying on God's grace I have for six years here sought to keep that promise.
>
> At the same service the congregation's members "promised both to labor in the ministry of the gospel and to give him, David Bowman, due honor and support."
>
> The petition makes me wonder what I have done or not done to relieve you of the obligation.

Earlier, on July 5, 1988, in a letter to the congregation, I wrote:

> These have been fulfilling years in many ways. But the days here grew long and hard as well. Some of those who invited me here turned away from me soon. For the past couple of years, I've been the object of an increasingly hostile campaign to which I remained silent. Many knew nothing; others only knew innuendo and rumor. Quite a number who had no axe to grind fell under this opposing influence. I believe mean-spiritedness lay at the heart of it, though other dissenters avoided that attitude. Doubtless my ministry has been flawed in one manner or another. But deserving of censure? Hardly.
>
> I am quite unapologetic about my ministry here. With the Lord's help, along with training and experience, I am both competent and caring. The previous year or two proved difficult, yet the constant sense of my call to ministry, the encouragement of many, and family support held me steady.

## Conflict and Resolution

Ministry in that parish proved both exciting and productive. It also exhibited obstacles and brought pain. The ministry began September 1, 1982, and concluded August 31, 1989, exactly six years to the day.

### Is It a Good Fit?

There may be two main ways to look at whether or not a particular minister fits into a specific parish. Of course, there might be lots of criteria to set side by side—education levels, cultural background, economic expectations, patterns within the Protestant spectrum, etc.

It might be said fairly that I was ill-fitted for UCUP, Tacoma, Washington, on two counts: gnostic/new age teachings vs. incarnational Christian faith and divergent attitudes on war and peace.

My predecessor, Rev. Pierce Johnson, along with some members of the congregation, were involved in a group with the psychiatrist, Carl Jung, as its absentee guru. This ideational foundation clashed with my own theological emphasis on the incarnate focus of Christian meanings.

There's a clear link between gnostic views, of which Carl Jung was a life-long student, and the development in our time of "new age." As Paul Vitz, in *Psychology as Religion: The Cult of Self-Worship*, writes, "The most historically important psychologist with major New Age links is Carl Jung." He goes on to say, "New Age systems can be clearly seen as a recrudescence of Gnosticism, in a form quite similar to its ancient manifestations."[3] So when I taught about our psychosomatic unity of human persons rather than about our souls attached to "a dying animal," this set off vibrations in certain quarters. Mr. Overman once in an aside complained that I never talked enough about angels.

Most people in the congregation knew nothing of this tension over "new age." Another subject caught the attention of some. These were folks with military backgrounds. I would say it's likely that a substantial portion of the financial backbone of the congregation came from offerings drawn from military pensions.

At that time, in the mid-eighties, the Cold War continued full bore. We spoke of ourselves as living at "Ground Zero" with the Boeing industry to the north, McCord Air Force Base to the east, Fort Lewis Army Base (the world's largest) to the south, and the Trident Submarine Base to our west. What more strategic location for the Russians to drop a large bomb?

3. Vitz, 120.

Tensions rose in this regard. I mention a couple: The Church Board complained that I wrote peace-oriented letters published in the Tacoma News Tribune as pastor of the church, when these should be identified as my own private views. Mr. Clint Cannon, a retired colonel, led the charge on this. I sought to come to terms with this concern by agreeing to identify myself as pastor of the church but offering my own views, not speaking on behalf of the parish.

Sundays close to patriotic holidays became an issue. A number of folk complained that not enough patriotic appeals issued forth in the liturgy and in the pulpit word. I tried to come to terms with this concern by liturgical elements and pulpit references on Sundays close to Memorial Day and July 4th. But these were regarded as too veiled or too couched in lack of "rah rah" rhetoric. The truth of the matter is, I usually took such occasions as calls for peace rather than celebrations of war. Two message titles on Memorial Day weekends were "The Harvest of Peace" (also Pentecost Sunday) and "Taking Jesus Seriously on Peace."

Take Sunday, May 29, 1983, for example, on "Taking Jesus Seriously" (on peace) from the pulpit I noted that Christians trust Jesus for peace in the life to come and inner peace while here on earth but when he says, "Blessed are the peace makers, for they shall be called children of God" (Matt 5:9), we enjoy "the stately cadence of the phrase, appreciate the sentiment expressed and then turn away never seriously to take his message of peace in the world."

I offered a few reasons why Christians may have ignored this dimension of Jesus' peace. We have (a)forgotten his own non-violent words and demeanor; (b)misunderstood Jesus' definition of the neighbor; (c)found the call to peace too impractical in a hostile world; and (d)find ourselves too loaded down by vested interest, i.e., our rewards from the military industrial complex. (This latter point may have hit home in a congregation well scattered with military pensions.)

I closed in this way: "The first Christian confession was 'Jesus is Lord,' not 'Jesus is Savior,' though that he is. Christians don't have to answer for some politician's view of peace, or some preacher's outlook either, but if Jesus is Lord then his will for peace in this world is binding. Let us not ignore it. It's likely to be the world's last remaining hope."

I do not regard that message to be unpatriotic. But it was not "for God and country" in the way a number of folk desired on Memorial Day. We took "a time of silence" to remember those afflicted by the scourge of war. That did not suffice.

So, there I was, caught between the "new age" folk on the one hand and the militarists on the other. During those six (very long) years I was enabled to carry out effective ministry on many fronts, but the clouds of conflict gathered.

On June 20, 1988, the Pastor-Parish Relations Committee received a letter signed by forty-three members asking that my pastorate be terminated in three months. The letter contained no specific complaints.

Perhaps it was just a bad fit. On the other hand, it provided the opportunity for vital ministry against the odds.

## Evaluating Ministry

Lots of Protestant congregations possess by-laws which speak of the Personnel or Pastoral Relations Committee. In the church where I experienced the most intense conflict over the time of the ministry, from 1982 to 1988, we called the body the Pastor-Parish Relations Committee (PPR). The object of the name pointed to a body which communicates on behalf of the congregation to the pastor and on behalf of the pastor to the congregation.

In my experience, the news of concerns from the congregation occupy the committee's time. The purpose of speaking to the congregation about the pastoral ministry in progress seldom occurs. Such was the committee at UCUP in Tacoma, Washington. This extremely active team conducted three congregation-wide evaluations and one mediatorial effort over the six-year span. In 1986 they brought in the services of a leading, now retired, United Methodist minister, Rev. William Ritchey, in order to evaluate the congregation. Briefly speaking about an extensive report, he found an active, growing congregation with a history of "I'll do it my way." He found a pastor (yours truly) providing "solid preaching, warmth to all, helpful in grief situations, working at church growth, with an ecumenical vision for the work of the church in community and world." But, said Mr. Ritchey, the pastor's "assertive leadership style has caused friction."

Then came the recommendations: Four years into ministry together, there is conflict which is not irreparable. He wanted the PPR Committee to report on the good news of the minister's work to the congregation and he suggested how to do this. He wanted the pastor (yours truly) to hone administrative and conflict management skills.

Many other recommendations were made, but this positive mediatorial effort for the most part lay dormant in file thirteen. The scene, if followed through on by all, might have improved. Instead the picture became more conflictual.

Other churches I served possessed more recessive, in some cases hardly active, PPR committees. Congregations with no strong tradition of such bodies scarcely understand its function. Sometimes the leadership skills needed for such an operation may not be present. Sometimes less formal groups in the congregation take on the role.

One thing is certain. Evaluation of ministry goes on all the time, most of it in private conversations over the phone, or these day by social media. It is a healthy situation where a recognized body tells the congregation about the good things of the minister's work and at the same time supportively assists the minister in dealing with complaints that arise.

## Working Together and Otherwise

Grinnell is a college town located centrally in the State of Iowa, about fifty miles east of the capitol, Des Moines. The Congregational Church, later to be United Church of Christ–Congregational (UCCC), occupies a geographical central place in town. J.B. Grinnell came from New York state to establish the town, the college, and the church. Legend has it that he's the one to whom Horace Greeley spoke when he said, "Go west, young man!"

The term, "town/gown," designates a distinction between the community and the campus. The distinction prevailed during the 1988–1994 period of my ministry there. The college, distinguished by its academic powers as a sort of Midwest "Ivy League" school, lay a mere couple of blocks away from the town center, but one seldom saw students walking those town sidewalks. The town and gown seemed to pass each other in the night.

What one would expect to be a cosmopolitan atmosphere did not seem available. The UCCC congregation included a few staff and faculty, including the college President, George Drake, and the Chaplain, Denis Haas, but scarcely any students. Consequently, in spite of geographical proximity, the international flavor of the campus did not permeate the life of the congregation.

In my 1991 Minister's Annual Report to UCCC in Grinnell I spoke of two lay women, members of the church, on staff as coordinators of education. Of Church School–Youth Coordinator, Oliva Wright, I said, "Oliva

CONFLICT AND RESOLUTION

accomplishes much in the time allotted; she is a doer and is fun to work alongside." And of Janis Peak, Adult Education Director, I said, "Jan provides skill, experience and personal rapport, which is of great value to the church." For four years we were a trio working in harmony. Oliva believes she not only made contributions but that it was personally therapeutic. Jan makes a taciturn comment, "I enjoyed working with you and Oliva."

But all was not harmonious in happy valley. When we arrived in Grinnell in 1988, in a sort of aside, a member of the Search Committee said, "Watch out for Sadie." I thanked him but indicated over-confidently that I could handle it. I was wrong!

One incident illustrates the problem. I decided that we should move from an 8½x11" Sunday bulletin format to an 8½x14" size. (I gained the approval of the appropriate committee.) A minor matter, really. Except Sadie objected. On shelves in the conference room, lined up in yearly order covering many decades, sat bound copies of previous years' bulletins. To change the format size would interrupt the alignment of those annual volumes. It would also, to some extent, alter the routine of Sadie. She objected. She objected strongly.

We moved to 8½x14" bulletins. But Sadie, a long-term member of the congregation, took her discontent out of the office, complaining over coffee to this and that person about that and this. She, a lovely hometown person, was in the driver's seat, so to speak. The minister? He could not criticize a member of the congregation. No way to ask for an administration change.

Reflecting on that scene I believe Sadie regarded me as a newcomer in an established pattern. If I did not rock the boat, all would be well. Change was unwelcome. Sadie had a long-standing web of influence in the congregation. I think she spoke often and negatively about my leadership. The truth of the matter: She was a Grinnellian and I was an interloper. The power rested in her court.

Clergy often feel they have more authority than actually exists. Authority requires kinetic power that can only be earned over a period of years. I knew of an Episcopal rector who newly moved in next door to the church. In the first week he walked over and rearranged the chancel furniture. Perhaps he had the authority, but he lacked the power. One year later he was gone. "It just didn't work out" the people said.

So, as late as January 1993, five years into this ministry, the Pastor-Parish Relations Committee annual report read, "The Pastor-Parish Relations

Committee expresses thanks to David for his excellent ministry and we are very supportive of his total program."

The old saying goes, "Don't believe everything you read." Indeed, there were boo birds quietly in the pews. I could hear the sounds of silence. The words of the critics were not on subway walls or tenement halls but they were spoken here and there in coffee klatches. It was time for a change. I reassembled my dossier and sent it out on the breeze. The Search Committee person's words had prophetic weight—"Watch out for Sadie."

## Promises! Promises! Promises!

Promise Keepers is a Christian organization for men. It is self-described as a body "dedicated to introducing men to Jesus Christ as their Savior and Lord."

It was founded in 1990 by Bill McCartney, then the football coach at the University of Colorado, in Boulder. Its most prominent event, called "Stand in the Gap," took place in Washington, D.C., October 4, 1997. Somewhere between 600,000 and 800,000 attended.

Ben Trell joined Promise Keepers sometime in the 1970s. I think I remember his attending the Washington, D.C., event and finding it inspirational. A leading member of First Congregational Church, Angola, Indiana.

During the six-year stint in Angola, I would sometimes turn to Ben to gain his insights on this or that. He seemed a thoughtful fellow and his Promise Keeper commitments seemed wholesome enough to support good churchmanship. One of those seven promises to keep, called a "core belief," read, "A promise keeper is committed to supporting the mission of his church by honoring and praying for his pastor."

The local church appeared to be moving well in the late 1990s. That is evidenced by membership growth, paid-up budgets, and well-planned efforts in motion to repair the sanctuary and restore the fine stained glass windows in time for the centennial celebration in the spring of 1999. Alongside that, I took leadership roles in local ecumenical efforts, engineered developments of Habitat for Humanity (HFH), and chaired the Steuben County United Way Board. But, unknown to me, ferment bubbled below the surface.

A local attorney and his wife during worship usually sat near the front of the sanctuary. I recall their first complaint to me: the recent bulletins during Pentecost season have been red in color and hard to read. Then one Sunday following worship, with no regret of visage or voice, they approached me at the close of worship to say they found my pulpit words without edification for them and they would be looking for another church home. Surprised, I wished them well and bade them goodbye.

Then the dominoes began to fall. The Trells were more than slightly impressed by the status of the attorney and felt included to be their friends. Another lay leader seemed susceptible to the commentary of Ben—and so on down the line. One afternoon it became clear to me that my presence and ministry were *persona non grata* to some of the congregation's lay leaders. Promises. Promises. Promises.

I was sixty years of age. Thirty-one years into pastoral leadership in the local church. I could have fought for my role. Instead, I came home and said to my wife, Dianne, "I don't want to do this anymore."

Soon afterward we shook the dust off our feet and moved to Adrian, Michigan, in retirement. And also to open a bookstore called, The Bookery.

## Create a New Hymnal

In 1990, the Iowa Conference Minister, Rev. Donald Gall, wrote me asking if I would serve on the newly forming UCC committee to create a new hymnal. Believing I had the poetic sense, the theological acumen, and a modicum of music ability, I answered yes.

A committee formed composed of clergy and laity, five of whom could play the ears off a piano or organ. The next three years, with twelve others, I spent time and energy coming to terms with the project. With the permission of my local church board, I pursued hymn development some thirty days a year.

Some important decisions needed to be made at the outset: First, would it be a joint UCC–Christian Church/Disciples book? (Much shared ministry went on between the two denominations, as it does to this day.) After an intense meeting of the two denominational committees and staff persons, the decision was made to go our own ways. Second, we searched for an editor and chose Arthur C. Clyde. Third, we listened carefully to presentations from a number of persons who embodied expertise in music and hymnology. The orientation to hymnology I remember best issued from Paul Westermeyer of Luther Theological Seminary, author of the magnificent *Hymnal Companion to Evangelical Lutheran Worship*. (The Lutheran hymnal appeared in 2006 and the companion in 2010.)

The general pattern of our work as outlined by our committee chair, Rev. James Crawford, pastor of Old South Church in Boston, involved breaking into various working groups—worship resources, hymnal format, various parts of the church year, etc.

All of us were united in our love of and appreciation for hymnic texts and tunes. I remember one occasion in Houston, Texas, when Linda Robinson of Plymouth Church in Seattle, Joyce Johnson of the Spelman College faculty and organist for First Congregational Church in Atlanta, Margaret Tucker, organist at First Congregational Church, Houston, and I assembled to choose hymns for the Advent section. We came up with an Advent text we liked but the tune options seemed desultory. Margaret stepped over to the piano. She said, "How about this?" She played as we sang the text. All three of us exclaimed, "That's it! What's the tune?" Margaret replied, "I just made it up." We urged her, "Play it again." She replied, "I couldn't possibly. I don't remember."

The committee engaged in many layers of research. Submissions of hymns arrived from many sources. In small groups we traveled around the country making presentations to regional groupings of UCC folk, explaining our process and goals and listening for ideas.

All went swimmingly except . . . the committee received from the staff a two-page listing of language guidelines designed to help create inclusive usage. All thirteen members agreed that language lay open for change. From that point divergence of views emerged between those who were determined to insert constant change and others, like myself, who believed that certain traditional hymns deserved to remain as previously known.

An example of the controversy appears in the hymn, "Beautiful Savior." In stanza two the traditional words say, "Jesus is fairer." This proved objectionable on the grounds of alleged negative racial overtones. The final book appeared with that line reading, "Jesus is sweeter," a saccharine substitute.

The major confrontation swirled around the word, "Lord." The editorial staff, led by Ansley Coe Throckmorton, General Secretary for Education and Publication, had determined to delete altogether the term, "Lord," from the new hymnal. (Ms. Throckmorton boasted a female crucifix on the wall of her office.) I voiced the opinion that unless we could find another one-syllable term that contained both the connotations of transcendence, as in, "Lord of creation," and intimacy, as in, "Precious Lord, take my hand," then we ought not to jettison it altogether.

## Conflict and Resolution

The thirteen-member hymn committee and staff met in Orlando, Florida, in January 1993. Immediately after that meeting three of us, Rev. Nancy Livingston, a Southern Illinois pastor, Margaret Tucker, previously mentioned, and I received notice of our dismissal from the committee. Flexible, but not flexible enough! We had asked that the committee be allowed to vote on inclusion of hymns and choice of language. Clearly the votes moving toward less rigid political correctness lay at hand. Such votes were not allowed.

Shortly thereafter the ten remaining members of the committee received commendations for completed work, even though much remained to be done. In the next two years, a five-person "editorial panel" completed the hymnal according to the specifications of staff. Only James Crawford, whose views coincided with the staff, remained in that group, and he no longer in the chair.

In June 1993, the UCC met by the flooded Mississippi River in General Synod at St. Louis, Missouri. A brief model hymnal, the term "Lord" absent, the delegates found in their packets. I joined Nancy Livingston and Margaret Tucker in circulating among the state caucuses to inform them of the issue about "Lord" in the proposed hymnal.

We managed to get a proposal on the floor of Synod—no mean task—to review the "Lordless" matter. Rev. Thomas Dipko, Vice President, United Church Board for Homeland Ministries, found the mike to explain the cogency of the decision to delete "Lord." He was roundly booed. In the subsequent vote the delegates by a 60 percent to 40 percent margin asked that the term, "Lord," be restored to the hymnal. In the panel's subsequent deliberations, the term found its home in seventeen of the 617 hymns, but only when in traditional hymns it referred to the second person of the Trinity.

When *The New Century Hymnal* saw the light of day in 1995 a humorous feature appeared in stanza three of the beloved, "Silent Night." Of course, "Son of God" read "Child of God" instead. In line three the traditional "Jesus, Lord at your birth," now read, "Jesus Christ at your birth." That's fine if one wishes to witness to Jesus, the Messiah. But without a comma after Jesus one is simply left to ask, "Jesus Christ at your birth" what?

James Crawford, chair of the ousted Hymn Committee, claimed that this would be "the first book on the new century shelf." Indeed, the hymnal portrays numerous sparkling qualities. But across the denomination congregation after congregation found the radical word changes too disruptive to accept.

Nancy Livingston had lamented in committee that while numerous language changes were justified, the proposal before us would not edify many loyal UCC folk in southern Illinois pews. The *Chalice Hymnal*, published by the Christian Church/Disciples moved assertively in the direction of inclusive language but in a way that did not leave traditional singers trailing in the dust. At Bethel Church in Manchester, Michigan, I worked with the committee to bring the *Chalice Hymnal* to the sanctuary. I believe it was well received.

In the Congregational Library on Beacon Avenue in Boston and in the Library at Lancaster Theological Seminary in Lancaster, Pennsylvania, one may find an "Alternate Report" on the process leading to the development of *The New Century Hymnal*, a report prepared by Margaret Tucker, Nancy Livingston, and me.

I found inspiration, enjoyment and camaraderie in the three-year process toward a new UCC hymnal. But, as indicated above, it had its bitter aspects as well. I was raised with Christians on the right who exhibited much rigidity; in denominational leadership of the hymnal committee I discovered on the left an equal sort of rigidity.

I close this reminiscence on a lighter side. On several occasions when the committee found itself in a restaurant together, somewhere in the room a family and friends at table began to sing "Happy Birthday" to someone. The committee members joined in song. It sounded as if the church choir had gathered. Then on a couple of occasions, one member, the late Jeffrey Radford, the keyboard man for Trinity UCC in South Chicago (Jeremiah Wright's church where the Obamas attended), found a piano in the restaurant. Then the service staff and patrons heard a whole new rhythmic version of the song. Happy Birthday indeed!

## Choose Your Predecessor (and Successor) Wisely

Once I investigated a parish church notice which read: "We are looking for a successor to Rev. Dr. So and So, who retired from this pulpit after 26 years." I read no further. Who would want to be his successor? The second person after Dr. So and So might thrive, but likely not the first. Such is the plight of replacing Garrison Keillor on "Prairie Home Companion." How do you succeed an icon?

## Conflict and Resolution

In every parish, other than a new-start or a close-down, one follows someone. Part of ministry involves dealing shrewdly with the brightness and the shadows he or she left. Much coffee klatch conversation involves comparisons with the predecessor. If he or she were a brilliant administrator and one struggles with the task, then that is a problem. If one pays a lot of attention to parish visitation, unlike the predecessor, people think the new person walks on water.

Well do I remember in my last year as minister in Pullman, Washington, persuading Louise Ashworth to be president of the congregation. Then I left for another pastorate. A ways into her leadership role, Louise informed me of the loss in death of her husband, U. S. Ashworth. When she called to ask if I would return to conduct the funeral, I replied, "Thank you, Louise, but that's not possible. You have a minister now. I will attend as a friend, but he's the one to lead the service."

There's nothing heroic about that behavior. It's just appropriate. To return to a former parish interferes with the development of relationships which the new clergy person needs time to make. Judicatories in denominations often help laity to be sensitive to those issues.

In my next parish, UCUP, my predecessor, Rev. Pierce Johnson, stepped over the line a couple of times. He agreed to return to conduct a funeral. He invoked the usual ritual words, "Well, I had a special relationship to that person." When lay people do not have educated perspective, the incumbent may appear too defensive. It was in this particular case. Fortunately, I never again encountered the problem anywhere else.

Much later in my ministry I appeared as an intruder to my successor. Let my notes from an incident tell the story.

On Sunday, February 20, I arrived home to find a call from a member of my former congregation on my answering service. He said that his relative was hospitalized, believed she was seriously ill, and wanted me to visit her and bring her Holy Communion. He did say he did not think it immediately life-threatening.

I then called the hospital. The patient told me of her serious, but perhaps open-to-help, situation. I made no promises to her.

Immediately I called my successor pastor to let her know about the patient's situation, so she could follow up. Angrily she claimed I was interfering in her ministry.

I called the patient on Monday and told her I would not be visiting her and that I had called the pastor about her.

Let me add, without saying exactly, what the caller and the patient said: The patient lived a rather reclusive life. She would not have asked the pastor to visit. She said she called me because of my "diligence in calling" on her during the time I was Interim Minister. (I made perhaps six visits to her house. She never acknowledged it, as she never had come to the door, save one time. Only now do I know that this ministry was valued.)

It came to my notice later that the pastor had contacted the Conference Office in Lansing to complain about my interference with her ministry. In retrospect I do not see how I could have acted more circumspectly.

I recall a pleasant experience in which I joined predecessors in celebration of parish life. In 1986, the CCUCC, in Pullman, Washington, celebrated its centennial. The minister, Rev. Peter Stevens, and Barbara Johnson, mistress of ceremonies, invited previous ministers to speak for ten minutes: Rev. Lincoln Wert (1941–1948), Rev. David Julius (1948–1960), Rev. Ted Edquist (1960–1970), and myself (1971–1982). As one may see, each of us had served for approximately a decade.

On this occasion all observed a miracle; each minister completed his remarks within the allotted ten-minute period!

## Youth Work Trip Again and Another Surprise

In the spring of 1989, we left Grinnell, Iowa, and traveled to Tacoma, Washington. By we I mean high school youth and adults from UCCC, where I had begun to minister in the summer of 1988.

While in Tacoma I had been active, as usual, with HFH. We made a connection: A refugee family we welcomed from Cambodia, the Tangs, would occupy a rehabilitated house and property owned by HFH.

In those days persons under eighteen were allowed to work on HFH sites. There's a certain enjoyment about tearing things apart. The youth, with hammers, crowbars, saws, etc., gutted said house. Before the work week closed, under the leadership of the HFH site manager, we even began to rebuild the house from inside out.

But now the surprise. Two adult leaders, became more than a little friendly. A problem! The woman wore a wedding ring given by her husband. She was the mother of two children awaiting her return in Grinnell. The above-mentioned relationship deepened. Another problem: The woman held a paid position at the church.

## Conflict and Resolution

Immediately after returning to Grinnell I learned that the new couple were (how shall I put it?) at opportune times hanging out together in a house down the street. Right away I told the woman that the relationship needed to cease or I would find it necessary to speak with the Church Council and request they ask her to step aside from her leadership position.

Well do I remember an evening meeting in my church office. The couple wanted me to climb down from my "moral high horse." I simply told them the behavior they modeled not only scared the horses but failed to set a Christian example for the young people of the church.

In a real sense, my ministry in Grinnell never quite recovered from this incident. On the one hand, I chose not to "blow their cover," since the woman did step aside. Meanwhile, she assured any number of people in the congregation that I met the criterion of a horse's ass.

Not long down the road, a divorce took place. Not long after that the new couple married. Lots of fine work on behalf of HFH took place, and a courageous, industrious family found a new home, but the week away provided an incubator for divorce rather than an encouragement to do counseling about a marriage doubtless fraught with problems. Is it not often true of life? First the fulfillment of purposes and next the unintended consequences.

## A House Divided Against Itself . . .

In the heart of Manchester, Michigan, stands an attractive edifice housing a United Church of Christ called Emanuel (the spelling, though unusual, is correct). I came there as Interim Minister in June 2004, and remained through January 2005.

This strong congregation of Evangelical and Reformed background suffered discord prior to my coming on the scene. John Korican, a veteran school principal and a leading member of the church, wrote:

> We were a church with a strong and large membership . . . the next Pastor did not measure up . . . The start of an added "Praise Service" further split the congregation with members leaving and a big drop in giving . . . Pastor Bowman agreed to accept our interim position . . . He went to the source of the problems and resolved the differences . . . We are a church on the mend and going forward in a strong positive manner.

Todd Mutchler, a local sheriff and chair of the Board of Deacons, wrote in the annual report to the congregation, regarding my ministry:

> His open, caring and thoughtful leadership has laid the foundation for Emanuel United Church of Christ to move forward. It has truly been a pleasure to work with a man of his talents and insights.

In a later letter of recommendation, Mr. Mutchler described the effort in more detail. He referred to "deep divisions within the congregation." Then he continued:

> Rev. Bowman immediately sought out the elected leadership of Emanuel and began the process of identifying issues within the church . . . One such issue was having two different services at Emanuel; one a "contemporary" service and the second the "traditional" service. Rev. Bowman . . . brought together a focus group consisting of church leadership and members–at–large to reach resolution on this issue . . . Emanuel has begun the healing process and the gap within the church has begun to narrow.

Doris Kittendorf, another leading member of the congregation, six months into the interim period, wrote a lengthy letter concluding with these words:

> We thank God that Pastor Bowman was willing to come to us and clear the way for the transforming power of the Holy Spirit to work within each of us. This good shepherd of the church has assuredly led us into greener pastures.

Having been the lightning rod of conflict in churches before, one is, of course, heartened to receive the approval of veteran lay leaders. But I know the very people who voiced these favorable comments were themselves, along with others, the ones who ran through the thickets with me to reach a better plateau.

As has been indicated above, a central conflict when I arrived lay between folk in the contemporary service and those in the traditional service. Each had staked out territory. Though I preferred the direction of the traditionalists, I could sense that the contemporary people brought with them energy, sincerity, and worthy goals. I participated energetically within both services. In the end both services continued. The difference? A growing sense that "those other folk" carried in them a worthy Christian vision and, since they are a part of us, we want to support their ministries.

## Conflict and Resolution

My personal worship preference lay in the direction of the more formal, liturgically endowed, public worship. The sanctuary housed a fine pipe organ and the organist, Susie Goodsen, knew how to open it up to God's praise. I have come to know, though, that the sound of the organ does not thrill and enrich everyone. As a pastor to all, I needed to keep this in mind.

Often I have thought that clergy receive both too much criticism and too plenteous applause. Each congregation brings its own set of problems to the table. These problems may include warring factions, wounds from previous pastorates that have not healed, and changing demographics in the neighborhood of the church building. The list could be much enlarged. Sometimes a pastor may bring the discernment and skills to address the issue at hand. Sometimes not.

I must say I appreciated the words of Todd Mutchler on the occasion of the farewell service for me after eight months as Interim Minister. The words came from Martin Luther King Jr.'s last speech before he was assassinated: "The ultimate measure of a person is not where he/she stands in moments of comfort and convenience, but where he/she stands at time of challenge and controversy." (Altered to make it gender inclusive.)

It is the core leadership of the congregation that makes the crucial difference. I enjoy the story of the congregation who came together in special business meeting to deal with the crisis of a sanctuary roof in sad need of repair. Everyone knew that the old gentleman in the back of the room, well-endowed with this world's wherewithal, carried the key vote. Late in the meeting he stood to voice the opinion that it might be best for the congregation to just let well enough alone and hope for the best. When he resumed his seat a piece of plaster fell off the ceiling striking the man on the head. A member sitting toward the front was heard to pray, "O Lord, hit him again." And the minister? He was praying too—in silence.

# On the Lighter Side

A Sunday School teacher was teaching the Golden Rule. "It means we are here to help others," she said.

A little girl raised her hand and asked, "What are the others here for?"

    LOYAL JONES, *More Laughter in Appalachia*[1]

---

1. Jones & Wheeler, *More Laughter*, 115.

## The Man with the Cane

PULLMAN, WASHINGTON, LIES NEAR the Idaho border, stashed among the rolling, winter wheat sewn, Palouse countryside. We served eleven years there. The incident happened on Maiden Lane, a street headed north from downtown.

He just held out his cane. Stepping off the sidewalk between parked cars, he simply held his cane parallel to the ground, extending it out into traffic. If I had proceeded, my car likely would have knocked the cane from his grasp. Or, perhaps, had he held it firmly enough, it could have damaged my right front headlight.

I later gathered that this unusual behavior was a daily *modus operandi*. He would walk down to the town center. When finished with his business, or whatever, he would do the cane extended procedure in moving traffic. Often the driver would stop. Then the elderly gentleman would simply open the passenger door and say, "A ride up the hill?" Usually he would be invited aboard.

So, sure enough, I invited him in. He clambered in, cane and all, and took his seat. As we accelerated up Maiden Lane, he began to tell me of his occasional attendance at a church further up the hill, adjacent to the university campus. He said, "I go to that church some times, but you can't hear a damn thing the preacher says." Did I reveal to him that indeed his chauffeur for the day was that culprit in the pulpit? No. I just drove on and deposited him at his door.

I knew exactly of what the old man spoke. On some Sundays he would shuffle in during the service and plop himself down in a pew on the outside aisle, about half-way up in the nave. He did not stay long. After a time, during the course of the sermon, with use of the cane, he would rise from the pew and head out, muttering aloud for most to hear, "You can't hear a damn thing he says." Of course, nearly everyone could hear his complaint, and I, the preacher, was speaking with microphone a good deal louder than the exiting worshiper.

His name was Henry Fletcher Rodeen, a man of Swedish descent. Once married, they had a son, but an early divorce meant he never did much fathering. He lived about half-way between the church and downtown. A sign nailed to the front porch of his house read, "Reflexology," which I learned to be some form of foot massage or manipulation designed to remove pain or discomfort. Since then I've learned he had other occupations: baker, watch repairer, jeweler. A student of foods, he claimed that pure beet juice resurrected him from a two-year stint in a wheel chair. A reporter interviewed him once. She titled her article, "Hobo Baker Turned Watch Repairer." When he climbed in my car that day, he just told me he did reflexology.

Moral of the story for preachers? Stop for all canes. O yes, and remember to speak up, even if you have a microphone.

## Pickings from "The Blackburn Patch"

During ministry years in Pullman, Washington, we might see as many as six faculty members from WSU English Department participating in the morning worship. People in that department were more likely to attend church than others. The anthropologists, for example, were noteworthy by their absence.

Given the experts in English syntax and rhetoric, I tried to be more than usually conscious of my words. When in the subjective mood, for example, one does not wish to utter, "If I was to go." I do remember with chagrin an after church moment when Robert Johnson, a certain twinkle in his eye, asked, "Do you always split infinitives?" The title for the morning message: "To Really Believe." Nowadays, of course, such splits have become commonplace.

One of the English professors, Charles Blackburn, nearly always in the pew of a Sunday, read the hymnal with a discerning eye. *The Pilgrim Hymnal* contained a lot of lyrics and tunes gathered from the 19th century. Charles knew that era well. You could see him eying the bottom of the page to spy out the poet involved.

## Parish, the Thought

Our church newsletter during that period opened its monthly pages to church members to voice their ideas or opinions. A few did. The above-mentioned, Charles, we asked to write precise, concise, fifty-word editorial prose per issue. He did so. At times he referenced literature, as with Emerson, Melville, etc. In humor, and other times in a more serious vein, he invariably produced prose worth reading.

We entitled these pieces, "The Blackburn Patch." Here find three harvestings from the "Patch."

Commenting on the UCC "Statement of Faith," primarily written in 1957 by Daniel Day Williams (representing the Congregational constituency) and Roger L. Shinn (representing the Evangelical and Reformed body), Professor Blackburn picks out the phrase, " . . . eternal life in his kingdom which has no end." He writes:

> The "Statement of Faith" recited some 30 or 40 Sundays a year in our congregation is a careful collage of profound theological ideas sifted through some 2,000 years of meditation. Any phrase may be seen as a placid surface beneath which lies the deepest reach of man's hopes and fears. An example, not quite fair, appears in the phrase "eternal life in his kingdom which has no end." Do we who sometimes do not know what to do on a rainy Saturday afternoon really want eternal life? Do we, born to distrust monarchy, really want to live in a kingdom? Do we temporal beings wearing watches understand something which has no end? While we can't stop to think for 2,000 years, still we had better think a little more and recite less easily.
> 
> Charles B.

In another "patch" Charles offers a piece of wisdom about what constitutes a reliable sort of faith, as follows:

> A sound test of a religion is the counsel it offers for getting through today. Only the present is reality, "the meeting of two eternities, the past and the future." A religion that consoles today by promising a golden tomorrow has failed to hear, "Take no thought for the morrow," or to understand the casual, "In my Father's house are many mansions. If it were not so, I would have told you." The meaning is, live today. A religion that depends upon either yesterday or tomorrow is not good enough for today.
> 
> Charles B.

And then receive an example of Charles' sly humor quite in touch with ancient writings and contemporary life as follows:

# On the Lighter Side

TELEGRAM TO JESUS (50-word night letter, collect)

Exploration of peace on earth is social action committee project here but everyone amazed and somewhat disheartened by discovering peace not only very controversial issue among Christians but also very confusing. Can we discuss peace without making enemies? Please help David help us understand each other in peace. Yours hopefully.

Charles B.

I guess I find it hard not to share just one more sample from "The Blackburn Patch." Early on in my ministry in Pullman, Charles wrote the following. It's a sort of prayer with twinkle in the eye and a twitch of smile of the corner of his mouth:

TELEGRAM TO JESUS—NIGHT LETTER (Collect)

New minister just completing first six months. As newness wears off strong metal shows underneath. Has great concern for all people in his parish. Our problem is adjusting to parish size—all God's green earth. Have read John 3:16 but have you any other suggestions?

Respectfully, Charles B.

Every church newsletter should have Professor Blackburn on the editorial staff. It would relieve the endless boredom.

## A Cold "Sitting" We Had of It

Every so often a representative from church pictorial directory firms will drop by church offices seeking to interest the parish in a new informative picture book.

These directories provide a service to the congregation as well as providing family photographs if the portraits prove worth the purchase.

In the winter of 1972–1973 we engaged a directory company for this purpose. For some reason the church furnace went on strike during the days scheduled for the photographs to be taken. It was so cold we could hardly stand the "sittings" in the Fireside Room. But with not a few good natured complaints, the photograph sessions per appointment proceeded to a successful completion. Well, maybe a few of the smiles appeared a bit frozen.

Then all we needed to do was await the arrival of the directories. Patiently, we waited. And waited. And waited. Then we made a telephone call. The message: "We're sorry to inform you that the directory company has gone out of business." What? Really? "So where are the directories?" we asked. Came the reply, "We have no idea."

I do not remember the search details. We discovered the directories had been completed prior to the firm going bankrupt. After diligent search, as with the Magi seeking the baby, we found our directories in a Texas warehouse. Eventually we received and distributed them.

At least we had not frozen for nothing. *C'est la vie*!

## Postlude

In a somewhat jovial mood, after eleven years as minister of CCUCC, in Pullman, Washington, my family and I were "pulling up stakes" and moving further west—to Tacoma, Washington. Hence the following in-house memo.

MEMO
To:      Selected friends. For in-house discussion only.
From:    David Bowman
Date:    July 23, 1982
Re:      Underground Rationale for Abandoning Pullman—in no order of priority and without much priority at all.

1. Bill Hall, so the rumor goes, is leaving Lewiston for Seattle. I simply could not imagine living in Eastern Washington without his "Lewiston Tribune" editorials to spark the mornings.

2. The rollers on my office chair keep falling off. Let's hope I have a new chair in Tacoma. Isn't there a colloquialism, "The wheels keep coming off"?

3. My supply of professional calling cards, thousands of which I ordered in 1971, is running low. Is that not a sign or omen?

4. They tore down the barn above Finch's Market. All the landmarks are passing!

5. Too many germs, viruses and other invaders were penetrating the Bowman household this spring; it's time to go somewhere else and try our fortune with a new batch.

# On the Lighter Side

6. This has been a rather extensive stay on a Horace Greeley–provoked trip west, beginning in Glasgow, Scotland, and proceeding to the New York Queens, Grand Rapids, Pullman, and now, Tacoma. Orient Express here we come!

7. The book and paper buildup in my church study began to threaten me. Each year I remain the concentric circle in which I work becomes smaller. I had visions of headlines reading, "Local Clergy Suffocates in Office Paper Pile." Leaving will force any pack rat to toss some items.

8. I was hit over the head by a pew pad. There was no apparent injury. But the buzzing in my head remains to this day. Don't tell anyone. They might come for me and put me in a padded cell.

9. We're leaving because, to coin a phrase, "Our place is going to the dogs." On the north side of our property the neighbors' two beasties bark at me when I'm innocently weeding my own garden. On the south side of the property, the odor of canine dung stinks to high heaven. We're fleeing the dogs!

10. Creatures whose ancestors crawled out of the water are instinctively called back to the shore? Pshaw!

Shalom!

Postscript: Perhaps only number eight requires explanation. A couple of years earlier we had a congregational meeting to vote on installing pads on the pews. My position—that it would be acoustically detrimental—went down to defeat. A stalwart member gave me a dirty look at the door. It was not a crushing defeat, but the whole matter left a bad taste in my mouth.

## Taking Things in Her Own Hands

I served a congregation in Grinnell, Iowa, 1988–1993—the UCCC, at Fourth and Broad Streets in the downtown. On any given Sunday morning there might be fifteen retired UCC clergy in the pews, the consequence of a large retirement facility, Mayflower Home, a few blocks away, founded by the Iowa Conference, United Church of Christ. It also happened that some agency had listed Grinnell as one of the best retirement communities in the nation. Dwight Johnson and his spouse, Elsie, learned about this welcoming feature and bought a retirement house there just for that reason, as Dwight proudly announced.

A significant number of our church members, clergy and lay persons, lived at Mayflower. One of those, Nina Richter, resided there, a widow of a pastor. The story I am about to tell revolves around her.

You may well imagine the scene. Long hallways with separate apartments for the retired residents. Quiet. No noise as in a dormitory or Greek house for students. Most conversations took place in appropriate muffled tones. Televisions and radios emitted sound generally confined to the apartment space. All except one.

I do not remember her name. It's probably just as well. She was an Episcopalian, which is neither here nor there. A self-confident person, outgoing and firm in her own convictions, she seemed a woman used to having her own way. On several occasions the management came to her saying, "Your neighbors find the noise level from your television intrusive. Please lower the volume." Many such entreaties. No satisfactory response. The annoying noise continued, day and into the night.

As a pastor, visiting in the community, I heard about the problem. I commiserated but she, the culprit, not a member of my flock, remained out of range of my advice. I knew her, greeted her, held light conversations, but nothing else.

Now I tell you the gospel truth. One day, in the brightness of daylight, not with stealth or any manner of concealment, this quiet, dignified widow of a UCC clergyman, Nina Richter, picked up a brick from her apartment, walked down the hallway, entered the offender's apartment and threw that brick through the television screen. As quietly as she went she then unhurriedly walked back to her own apartment and shut the door.

Much of the aftermath is lost to history. But I can tell you that the news spread, as they say, like wildfire. "Did you hear what Nina did?" . . . "You mean that quiet, dignified, Christian woman upstairs?" . . . "What?" . . . "Really?" . . . "Can you believe it?"

Certainly, the administration must have remonstrated with Nina. Were there reparations? Even law suits? Who knows. But those matters miss the point of the story. One day Nina had had enough. She took matters in her own hands. The result? Quietness! Blessed quietness! And up and down the hall in various apartments a keen observer might have seen smiles of satisfaction. And under his or her breath some retiree said, "You go, girl!"

On the Lighter Side

## The Parish Potluck

Garrison Keillor, erstwhile story teller on Prairie Home Companion, frequently mentioned potlucks at the Lake Woebegan Lutheran Church. Prominent on the menu were tuna hot dish and lime Jello with cottage cheese.

Reference to such dietary sophistication usually evoked laughter. That came before pointing up the main entrée—lutefisk—a Norwegian favorite. Doubtless the scent of it lingered, wafting up to the sanctuary on Sunday morning.

It is one of the miracles, for the most part unreported, that more people have not died of food poisoning from parish potlucks. The local sanitary supervisors, not being apprised of these culinary gatherings, do not appear to check on this, that, and the other, as they do at restaurants. One blanches to think of all the unsanitary kitchens in which various dishes are thrown together at the last minute by soiled hands in germ-laden pots. But for the most part it tastes good and leaves the partaker well fed. And feeling well. That's the miracle.

My wife, Dianne, and I nearly always looked forward to parish potlucks, since almost without exception the food laid out buffet style on long tables appeared well-prepared and attractively presented. Sometimes folk with last name A–M are invited to bring salads, while those N–Z folk bring desserts. Or some such arrangement. Often someone who has, "killed the fatted calf," brings the meat dish, carnivores that most of us remain.

The church I served twice in interim capacities, Bethel Church, hosts annual Sauerkraut Suppers, which draw 600 or so people. Organized to the hilt, folk wait in the sanctuary until their number is called, their stomachs growling for the feast they are about to enjoy. Food is prepared from "scratch"—sauerkraut with German sausage, mashed potatoes, gravy, apple sauce, and the German spätzle. Homemade pies are in abundance. This being a widely-advertised event, the "sanitary supervisors" from the county would make a preliminary visit to make sure all food was at the correct temperature, etc. This is a vast improvement on potlucks.

I said we nearly always looked forward to potluck dinners. Nearly always, I said. I do hesitate to mention one exception by name, but if I leave out the nomenclature, the other parishes I have served will come under suspicion. So full disclosure.

I refer to UCUP in Tacoma, an amalgamation of UCC and United Methodist. Ironically enough, the founding pastor, Jeff Smith, gained fame on television as the Frugal Gourmet, presenting all sorts of delectable dishes. (Parenthetically, he also wrote a column as a restaurant critic in the Tacoma, Washington, newspaper. Rumor has it that managers detested his pestering, taste-testing arrival, as he would send the dish back if it were not exactly to his specifications.)

Anyway, the congregation there gathered with some regularity for potlucks. Dianne and I would look at each other with despairing eye. We knew all too well what would come to the table. I tell you honestly, dear reader, each dish looked as if it has been pulled from the back of the refrigerator after weeks of incubation, having had time to sprout mold and long wispy hair. The eye did not deceive. The taste co-mingled with the appearance, making it necessary to escape surreptitiously to the restroom on the way scraping off the alleged food in the trash can. Upon arrival at home—Pepto-Bismol, Tums, etc. Of course, I exaggerate to make the point.

Surely God will excuse the subterfuge when the pastor on the way out assured Mrs. so-and-so of how much he enjoyed her well-aged goulash. After all, pastors seek to nurture, even in the throes of gastronomic distress.

## The Elevated Ghosts of Bethel

Upon entering an interim ministry at Bethel Church, Manchester, Michigan, I discovered that the church elevator, on its own time clock, opened and closed of its own accord.

The following is my "minister's minute" in a light-hearted vein for the June 2003 "Bethel Newsletter."

> One cannot help but notice that the church elevator door opens and closes of its own accord. There must be some electronic explanation for this. Or is there not? Oooooo!
>
> I suppose, as a relative newcomer, I take note of the peculiar antics of the elevator more than church veterans. During my recent visit to the women's group meeting in the dining room the elevator twice opened and closed of its own accord. Nobody in the room, other than myself, seemed to pay any attention.
>
> Upon inquiring into this strange phenomenon I was told, "The problem has been explored on several occasions leading to no explanation or change in the situation." Does it only happen in some phase of the moon? Does it open and close when nobody is around or only when people are present? And how would we answer that last question?

## On the Lighter Side

The good book says, "We are surrounded by a great cloud of witnesses" (Heb 12:1), but it fails to mention they ride church elevators.

The east wall of the dining room features the visages of ministers who participate in that "great cloud of witnesses." In my mind's eye, I see one or more of them stepping off the elevator to walk around, visiting the premises, checking to see if the current membership continues to uphold "the faith once entrusted to the saints" (Jude 1:3).

In spite of these pious thoughts of "Rev." visitations, it is reported that some rational people, not given to entertaining apparitions, while visiting the church building late at night, on hearing the elevator open and close, left the building earlier and more hastily than expected.

Actually, it seems to me a rather comforting thought to imagine some of the saints buried in the adjacent "kirk yard" paying a visit to the friendly confines of the towered church to pray for us, hoping that we too will pass on the faith in the same measure they have passed it on to us. And then when on that mission, they may enjoy the opportunity of an elevator ride folk of their era never experienced.

At any rate I know there's lots more to Bethel than meets the eye. There exist rich, deep-down things. More than eye or ear can ever tell. Things both human and divine. More mysterious even than the self-actuating elevator.

P.S. It was reported at the last Church Board meeting that the elevator had been repaired. Then someone stated it still opened and closed of its own accord. So, keep riding! And know this comforting thought: You are never alone!

## "The Lost Chord" Revisited

During 2003–2004 and 2007–2008, and briefly in 2005, I served as Interim Minister of Bethel Church, Manchester, Michigan. I had the privilege of working alongside Mary Sue Moore, Organist and Choir Director. She may be described as smart, industrious, fun-loving but no nonsense, musically skillful, accountable, and dedicated. Yes, all of the above.

## Parish, the Thought

In coordination with Mary Sue, one soon learned the necessity of planning services well in advance. She did and she expected others to do likewise. She knew the Bethel Church landscape, so one could glean from her lots of insights when stepping into the arena. Her wide-ranging knowledge grew from her vigorous participation in church life, including a green thumb dedication to keep the grass and extensive shrubbery in front the church building in fine condition.

When I prepared to leave Bethel in August of 2008, I told Mary Sue of my special appreciation for the song, "The Lost Chord," by Arthur Sullivan: "Seated one day at the organ, I was restless and ill at ease . . . " (Sullivan wrote the music in 1877 while seated beside his dying brother, Frederick.) Using the words of Adelaide Anne Proctor, the song "eclipsed in a few months in its sales all the songs of England for over forty years." [2]

An homage to Frederick, the text portrays a musician's near despondency until the music lifts him to a vision full of hope:

> It may be that Death's bright angel will speak in that chord again;
> It may be that only in Heav'n I shall hear that grand Amen![3]

I don't remember the sequence exactly. Perhaps Mary Sue asked me what anthem I would like on the last Sunday of my ministry at Bethel. Did I say, "The Lost Chord"? At any rate, Mary Sue put her pen to paper or her fingers to the computer keys and came up with a new text under the title, "The Pulpit Word," the words I often placed in the Sunday bulletin in place of "Sermon." Not exactly appropriate for the worship time, it was sung at coffee hour by the choir, as follows: Seated one day in his office with a ball point pen in hand,

> Rev'rend Bowman wrote his sermon; scriptures at his command.
> He knew that what he was writing next Sunday would then be heard.
> So he put the pen to paper and he wrote the great Pulpit Word.
> And he wrote the great Pulpit Word.
>
> Thoughts flooded his head willy-nilly, like the storm which follows a calm.
> And he worked at a fev'rish tempo that slowed when he read a Psalm.
> He must avoid pain and sorrow, but not overcome with strife.
> His message must get approval from his discerning wife.

---

2. Sullivan & Flower, *Sir Arthur Sullivan*, 114.
3. Ibid., 113.

## On the Lighter Side

At last he linked all his ramblings into one perfect piece.
The pen fell away from his fingers; his efforts then did cease.
He had sought to fill up the message with wisdom line by line.
It came from his heart, mind, and soul, in words that were divine.

It may be that angels in heaven will know of that message heard.
It will be that people of Bethel soon shall miss that grand Pulpit Word.
It may be that angels in heaven will know of that message heard.
It will be that people of Bethel soon shall miss that grand Pulpit Word.

# Close to Home

I believe that they[ministers] are called . . . to consider the lilies of the field, to consider the least of these my brethren, to consider the dead sparrow by the roadside. Maybe prerequisite of all those, they are called to consider themselves, what they love and what they fear, what they are ashamed of, what makes them sick to their stomachs, what rejoices their hearts.

Frederick Buechner, *Telling Secrets: A Memoir*[1]

---

1. Buechner, *Telling Secrets*, 38.

## Discovering the Frontiers of Ministry

DURING MY YEARS IN theological school, though not yet ordained, I was thrust into weekend ministry. Lying between our apartment and the seminary on the Paseo in Kansas City, Missouri, lay a small, brick building housing an edition of the Cumberland Presbyterian Church. I offered Sunday ministry there for a while.

The Cumberland Presbyterian Synod of Kentucky separated from its parent body in 1813. These folk sought clergy more on fire with the gospel, if less educated. They squirmed under some of the edicts of the Westminster Confession and they participated in the revivalism occurring on the frontier at the time. The expression in Kansas City, represented one of the more western extensions of the denomination. Its revivalistic heritage may have been a factor in inquiring of a Church of the Nazarene seminary if they had a fledgling pastor on the horizon.

On my shelves, among scads of hymnals, I still own a copy of the Cumberland Presbyterian Hymnal, published in 1956. It contains perhaps the most extensive section of readings, confessions of faith, etc., I have ever seen in a hymnal. Among its hymns one finds "Great is Thy Faithfulness," a hymn absent from most Protestant hymnals at the time, but now— returned to favor.

One other Sunday preaching station I remember—a United Methodist Church located somewhere in the Missouri country side. My wife, Dianne, and I journeyed to that white board building each Sunday over a period of time. The ritual included an invitation to Sunday dinner with a parishioner. Most of these occasions fade from memory. Only one Sunday clearly remains.

Dianne remembers features of the occasion that slip my mind. She remembers that the father, a very soft spoken, unassuming person, was alleged to hold an earned PhD. On a more mundane level she recalls that no furniture adorned what might be called the living room. Instead, there were three beds, all neatly made. At table the hostess served mashed potatoes thickened with flour, without milk. Liver and lemonade rounded out the main course.

No shame exists in all that. This couple and their children labored under the canopy of poverty. They shared their home and table with us. But it's what happened at the close of the meal which sticks in my mind.

The couple and children invited us to sit at a roughhewn donut shaped table stationed over a hole in the floor. When we finished eating, the next moment remains fixed in my memory: the family began to scrape from their plates the left overs. Where? Into the darkened hole in the center of the table over the hole in the floor. What became of the leavings in that unusual garbage disposal, we never knew.

I know you think this incident is just a figment of my imagination. False. I saw it and remember it.

O Lord, bless now this food of which we're about to partake, including that later to be discarded through the hole in the center of the table. Amen.

## A Little Elbow Room, Please

Traditionally, in the Protestant tradition, the manse, or parsonage, lay next door to the church building. In times when transportation provided less mobility the adjacent location made lots of sense. Also, in the tradition, the pastor's house came along with salary and benefits as part of the remuneration package.

How this has changed! Currently the pastor of a congregation I served lives fifty miles from the church building. In contemporary life many, perhaps most, congregations do not own housing for their resident clergy. Many clergy in the parish prefer to receive a housing allowance. Several reasons influence this consideration: First, in days when home ownership enabled one to build up equity, this proved a form of investment. (Since the economic down turn in 2008 this factor seems less inviting.) Second, pastors' families often wish to arrange and decorate a home in their own fashion, without the interference of a parish property committee. Third, the cost of moving clergy from pillar to post increased to the point where church budgets could ill assume the burden. This fact led to longer incumbents in the parish even in judicatories of a hierarchical sort, such as the United Methodists.

Speaking for myself, I never wished to live where I could look out my bedroom window and see the church building. Why? Simply because it's difficult enough to vacate one's momentary concerns from the person's situations and challenges of the parish without constant visualization.

I recall, with a hearty sigh, when I could drive away from the Grand Rapids Park Church parking lot and head west to Comstock Park some eight miles to the west. Not that the parish burden rested too heavily, rather I felt the need for overnight respite with home and family.

In other locations a certain distance obtained. In Pullman, Washington, we purchased a house across town. In University Place, Tacoma, Washington, we built a house about six lots from the church building, with a thick forested barrier intervening. The same general separation obtained in Grinnell, Iowa, and Angola, Indiana. In these latter situations I enjoyed the proximity that enabled me to walk from home to church and back.

Always I kept my main office or study in the parsonage. There I could be free to read, write the weekly message, and do parish planning. In the church office, where I enjoyed secretarial assistance, the general interactions of the parish took place, including counseling from time to time.

I suppose the main difference for me in these two locations is this: In the home study I could think and pray. In the church study I was there to do various ministries.

Even as I write this I realize that in going home I never really left the parish at the door. True, but surrounded by my library, the study at home always felt a bit like a retreat.

Everyone has his or her *modus operandi*. The pattern described above comes not as a recommendation; rather it's simply a description of what felt natural to me.

## No Casual Chat

There they sat in our living room. Two couples. The men, ordained clergy, were colleagues of mine. My wife, Dianne, and I had no clear idea why they had asked to gather. We knew each other but not on a "chum" or close friend basis. No cordial afternoon chat this. But what?

The agenda soon became clear: unwanted pregnancy. Four children already peopled the household of one of our guest couples. Dianne and I awaited in a few months the arrival of our third child. The couple in question. Did they have one or two children at that point? No talk of the weather. No cracking jokes. The subject was joined.

Why unwanted? Perhaps the expectant mother suffered from serious health issues? Maybe they had discovered through amniocenteses that the fetus showed definite signs of malformation? The mother-to-be was aging? Finances made a new mouth to feed a matter of deep distress? The answer to all of the above questions, and such ilk? No. It just seemed an inconvenient time. This pregnancy occurred out of sync with any family plans.

The conversation took place in order to gain the moral support—and the morale embrace—of these two colleague couples. In order to find the spiritual and psychological means to welcome a new son or daughter into the family? No. To hear words of approval toward ending the pregnancy? Yes.

The other couple flashed the green light. They assured the couple in waiting that an abortion would surely serve the best interests of the family. After all, this fetus did not yet bear the full requisites of a human being. So this should not be regarded as killing. And since it's important for children to be wanted, why not wait for a more opportune time? Such rationales tumbled out toward the pregnant couple.

Then Dianne and I began to speak. Dianne remembers, as a mother-to-be, how offended she was that they would have the audacity to come to our home and present themselves in this way, knowing that she was pregnant. We flashed yellow and red lights. We indicated that our faith tradition pointed toward another option—the loving welcome of a newborn, whether planned or unplanned. I noted that all the properties of a fully developed human being resided in the one maturing in the womb. How then can this be regarded as less than killing? This case involved not an alternative, but a destiny.

I believe the abortion took place. That was 1970. The Roe vs. Wade Supreme Court decision lay three years away. But already Planned Parenthood offices and other sites stood ready, behind closed door, to offer the requested services.

A short time later the Senior Minister used the newsletter to call attention to Senate Bill 1260, "A Bill to Authorize the Termination of Pregnancy." He asked members to contact their senators in Lansing, saying, "The time is past due for antiquated abortion laws to be revised." He failed to give any Christian rationale as to why legal prohibitions had become obsolete.

Abortion reform, so-called, moved forward—or backward—in those days. Petitions requesting signatures in favor of liberalizing the law appeared even at church doors. Few appeared willing to stand at the church door asking for signatures. Rather the announcement read: "The petitions will be found on tables near the various exits."

Later on, on May 23, 1971, the local TV station conducted an interview "concerning the moral issues surrounding abortion." The father-to-be of the child under discussion in our living room and I appeared "in order to discuss this vital and current issue." Our dialogue reflected stances taken in our home a year earlier. Of course, we spoke as professional clergy, not as involved parents.

In 1973, the Supreme Court ruled. The petitioners had their way. Millions of legal abortions later, the intense conversation continues. No casual chat.

## The Pastor's Wife: A Tradition Modified

My wife, Dianne, is a skilled musician. Since music runs in the family on her mother's side, a portion of the expertise lies in her DNA. Cleo Murphy, Dianne's mother, concluded her formal schooling at eighth grade at age fourteen. She married and rode off into the sunset with a twenty-seven-year-old preacher, Ezra Hendley. She had no formal education in music, but she had rhythm in her bones and music in her head, giving her lots of ability to lead church choirs, which for decades she did indeed.

The role of the pastor's wife, in tradition, contains certain prescribed rituals. Early on, Dianne indicated she considered herself like other members of the congregation and would fit in where she wished to make a contribution.

I well remember Esther Ann Shaw exiting the church door in Pullman, Washington, on a Sunday morning following worship. She said, "We will look forward to see you and Dianne at the women's gathering his afternoon." I replied, "I'm afraid you only hired one pastor." By this I meant, in a somewhat jocular vein, that I had no idea if Dianne would wish to attend and the event was not necessarily a part of her job description. Esther was offended. Later I apologized for my curtness, even though I had stated a truth that Esther failed to grasp, given her view of the traditional role of the pastor's wife.

Whenever we landed in a new parish I hoped the choir director's position awaited Dianne. Sometimes, yes, and other times, no. In the large parish where I was ordained, Park Church in Grand Rapids, Michigan, Dianne participated in the choir under the direction of organist/choir director, George Shirley.

When we came to Pullman, Washington, the position of Choir Director soon opened for Dianne. She led the choir for most of the eleven years of our stay there. She worked alongside organist, Lewis Magill, a member of the congregation, and the Chair of the English Department at WSU. Then came Myung Ja Kim, holding a doctorate in organ, whose husband, Yu Sam, pursued advanced studies at WSU. Then came Susan Billin, a fine musician.

Dianne experienced one memorable moment working with Dr. Magill. He sometimes came to Sunday morning service a bit snookered. On this particular Sunday in Advent, the United Methodist choir joined us for a special presentation of Buxtehude's, "Unto Us a Child is Born." It was first presented at our church with the Methodist choir director directing. They then went to the Methodist church for a presentation. Sure enough, Dr. Magill had already over indulged. When it came time for the music to begin, he began playing in the wrong key. In spite of that, the choir carried on successfully.

Thereafter, in three parishes of approximately six-year duration each, Dianne's role was more episodic. At UCUP, Tacoma, Washington, Dianne played scarcely any musical role, as the director and organist were already in place. Then later in Grinnell, Iowa, once again Dianne soon began to lead the choir, accompanied for several years by an excellent organist, Barbara Zacheis, on a good Allen organ. When we came to Angola, Indiana, we found the choir led by the director of choral music at the local junior high school. Initially Dianne sought to fit into the choir, but soon it became clear that the director was threatened by Dianne's musicality. Dianne returned to the pew for the remainder of our time there.

Another ten years lapsed before Dianne led a choir. When we left Adrian, Michigan, where we had retired, Dianne sold or discarded her music library, thinking that activity past. Attending Immanuel Lutheran Church in Saratoga, California, our new location, they announced the current search for a choir director. I, no longer an active pastor, nudged Dianne saying, "Throw your hat in the ring." She did. The Search Committee, about to decide on a candidate that barely pleased them, invited Dianne to lead a choir rehearsal. Immediately the committee decided: "She's the one!"

As I write Dianne is in her tenth year in that congregation. There's a good pipe organ in place, played upon well by Sophie Chang for nineteen years and currently by Elisabeth Pintar. Dianne's carefully chosen anthems presented by a seventeen-voice choir nearly always enhance the service. Her ability to hear the melody and the harmonies makes it possible during practice to sort out the anthem. She says, "Sing it this way." And then we do. I know. When I'm not off filling some pulpit, I'm usually an on-tune member of the bass section.

"Sing Hallelujah, not Hallalujah," she says, and we do—sometimes. "Don't slide up to that A," she says. And we plop down in the midst of the note—sometimes. Line upon line, precept upon precept, we listen and usually get it. In so doing, Dianne fulfilled the definition of famed church musician, Erik Routley, "A musician is an artist employed by the church who hopes to be able to give what he or she has for the edifying of the church's people."[2]

## Serendipity

On a Sunday morning in December 2003, Dianne and I headed north out of Adrian, Michigan, for a Christmas gathering of family in Lapeer, Michigan. We had no particular plan to attend worship, though we agreed we would seek to find a likely place along the way.

Turning off State Route 127, seeking a short cut northeast through the countryside, we came to an intersection marked Bethel Church Road. Dianne mentioned she saw a church around the corner. I replied I had heard of a UCC in this area but had never been able to locate it. We turned the corner and found Bethel Church.

When we entered, the sanctuary was packed. We sat on folding chairs in the back. The service had only begun. Soon children and young people began coming up the stairs and past us toward the front of the chancel. Some fifty or sixty of them. Amazing! A church crowded with young folk!

We had happened in on the Sunday of the Christmas Program. The lay education leaders were in charge. Skits, songs, and readings ensued. Next to us an effusive, talkative fellow offered a running commentary on the

---

2. Routley, *Church Music*, 140.

proceedings to a woman next to him. I would come to know it was Rev. Richard Hardy, the current but outgoing minister.

In the course of the service, it was revealed that Rev. Hardy in January would hold his last service as pastor of the congregation. Dianne suggested I might speak with Larry Guenther, Congregation President, to indicate my availability to lead services until an Interim could be found. Sort of an interim Interim.

On a January Sunday we found ourselves back in worship at Bethel. This time we entered upon Confirmation Sunday. The pastor planned to lead the service, his next to last time before departure to a new pastorate in Berea, Ohio. The Confirmation Sunday had been moved from May back to January so that Rev. Hardy, their mentor, could lead them toward membership.

The morning did not go as planned. During a baptism prior to the service Rev. Hardy had fallen ill. Duane Kuebler took him to the hospital in Saline. A lay leader, Garry Schleicher, led the service. One by one confirmands confessed their faith and indicated why they wished to be members of the church. One of them said he represented the eighth generation at Bethel. (We were to discover such continuity in this German background congregation was not unusual.)

Dianne and I were seated up toward the front. It came time for the congregation to confess its common faith. Usually the Apostles' Creed escaped the lips of the congregation. But today, this Confirmation Sunday, the Statement of Faith of the UCC appeared in the bulletin. Lots of folk began to say, "I believe in God the Father, maker of heaven and earth . . ." while some were reading the bulletin and saying, "We believe in God, the Eternal Spirit, Father of our Lord Jesus Christ and our Father and to his deeds we testify. . ." *Glossolalia* in a UCC Church!

I realized that a certain confusion reigned. The pastor was away. So, without much deliberation, I simply raised my voice and continued from the UCC Statement, "He calls the worlds into being . . . " A few seconds later we were all on the same page, as it were, and literally. Without meaning to take leadership in the congregation, I had done so.

That service, that moment, hinted of days to come.

## From Kiev to Adrian on the Wings of Song

Roger McMurrin, a college friend of Dianne and me, soloed in song at our wedding. Later on, he led music at Coral Ridge Presbyterian Church in Florida. Even later, Roger and his wife, Diane, I know not how, found themselves in Kiev, Ukraine. To their amazement, they found there a tradition of sacred music that survived the Soviet era and a residue of the fine musicality embedded in the DNA of the people.

In the post–Soviet period, Roger and Diane built a Christian ministry centered around sacred music. They assembled a large choir and orchestra and led them on a number of tours to churches in the United States.

So in due time, Dianne and I agreed to make all the arrangements necessary to host 150 choir and orchestra members from Ukraine. A myriad of plans ensued, including private housing for pairs of musicians. We received lists of the musicians by name. It turned out that any individual might have several spellings of his or her name. This proved baffling when seeking to assign the folk to host families.

It was required of me that I raise $10,000 in donations to meet the traveling expenses of the musicians. I raised $13,000. Large donations came from Merillat Industries, a prominent Christian entrepreneur in Michigan, and from David Hickman of United Bank and Trust Company. Lots of ecumenical support developed.

Hundreds of small hospitalities and responses took place. Even non–church families opened their homes. We discovered that many of the musicians owned little warm clothing—a surprise considering the temperatures in Ukraine. Several host families provided winter outfits for them. One of the bass soloists, a rotund man in his middle years, weighed down with health problems, required a hospitality house to himself. He ended up at our house for a while, his frame stacked upon a couch in our living room. He had trouble warming up, so I brought him an oversized sweater from my closet. Amazingly, it fit. He kept it. Dianne says he prized it "as if he'd won the lotto."

A 600–person ecumenical gathering assembled on a Sunday afternoon in the St. Dominic Chapel of Siena Heights University in Adrian, Michigan. Some had come across the state by bus load. Briskly, Roger stepped forward and in characteristic bold style raised his arms and baton. Music Ministry Kiev broke into orchestrated song. The universal sounds of refined, inspired Christian music filled the chapel. No praise band stuff this. Bach and Handel would have been proud to be in the audience to hear their compositions, and of their ilk, performed. The Ukraine musicians and the Michigan listeners joined in moments of profound praise to God.

The next morning the multitude assembled. Host families and musicians saying their goodbyes—smiles, waves, prayers, and on to the next venue, all with memories of a fine occasion.

# The Parish Church Building

> We would be building; temples still undone
> O'er crumbling walls their crosses scarcely lift,
> Waiting till love can raise the broken stone,
> And hearts creative bridge the human rift.
>
> PURD E. DEITZ, *"We Would Be Building"*[1]

---

1. Dietz, *New Century*, 607.

## Going to the Chapel to Get Married (The Marriage Mill)

SITTING IN MY CHURCH office at First Congregational, UCC, in Angola, Indiana, every so often I would look through the window to see a couple, perhaps holding hands, looking around the attractive chapel grounds. I would interrupt my work in order to go greet them. Inevitably I encountered a twosome who once upon a time said marriage vows in that chapel.

In 1949 this beautiful stone chapel, constructed behind the parsonage located several blocks away, came to pass. On May 15 of that year a dedication ceremony took place naming it the Humphreys Memorial Chapel, after Rev. John Humphreys, who served from 1904 to 1943, a remarkable 39 years.

In 1989, forty years after the chapel's construction, large machinery moved it to a more accessible location behind the church building. Interior renovation and landscaping around the chapel accompanied this move.

Over the years, literally thousands of wedding vows rattled around the chapel walls. Angola served as a marriage mecca, being a few miles from both Michigan and Ohio. Couples came from Michigan or Ohio where blood test waiting periods held sway. On the central plaza of Angola, the couple bought rings from one of several jewelers, walked over to the Court House for the blood test and license, and then traveled a couple of blocks for a chapel wedding. Accurate records record thousands of weddings per year. The usual Saturday schedule indicated vows at fifteen-minute intervals. (It is rumored that some of the income from these many weddings lined the pastors' pockets over the years.)

## The Parish Church Building

Finally, at an annual church meeting, J. Quentin Smith stood up and said, "Enough is enough!" He reminded the congregation it was not a commercial marriage center and the time to cease and desist had come.

No minor decision that. The church had become accustomed to live off the wedding revenue. Now membership giving at a much higher level needed to begin.

There followed soon a clergyman who proclaimed no interest at all in conducting multiple weddings. He had other fish to fry.

During my six years in Angola, I officiated at a few weddings. Angola had long since ceased to become a magnate for quickie knot tyings. My own position on availability made that even more unlikely. I insisted on at least two counseling sessions over a two week period. I also explained that two important events took place in a Christian marriage service involving promise and prayer: The promise needed to be expressed in terms of permanence, and the prayer after the vows, offered by the clergy person, required a sense that the couple joined silently in the petition and not just listened in non-committal fashion. These stipulations, quite legitimate I believe, caused secular couples to search elsewhere for wedding site and officiant.

Often I wondered, "What percentage of those thousands of quickie weddings held in Humphreys Memorial Chapel lasted? And how did that percentage stack up when compared to those well-planned, surrounded by family, nuptials?" Of course I never knew. I can report that those who came back to the scene of their vows seemed happy for the memory.

### Parish versus Mortuary

Where we lived on Manor Drive in Grinnell, Iowa, offered a noteworthy context. At the top of the rise lived a physician, next door down the hill resided the local mortician. We, the clergy family, lived next door at the bottom of the slope. An appropriate chronological progression—failed surgery, casket purchase, last rites.

But I come to speak to you mostly about the mortician. The Smith Funeral Home in Grinnell had, there's no other say to say it, a monopoly on death. Evidence? Just check the local telephone directory in the yellow pages under "Funeral." What do you see? Smith Funeral Home, 1103 Broad Street.

When "the death angel swooped down" on that college town in Poweshiek County, the Smith folk took charge. And boy were they in charge! Like every other mortuary I have known, they preferred the services take place in their chapel rather than the church sanctuary where the deceased person might have worshiped God for decades. Parenthetically, mortuary chapels used to have an electronic organ that produced tremulous sounds offered up by an erstwhile musician wearing mittens. Now these same chapels provide any sort of music, from country to operatic, over a speaker system. No funeral chapel I have ever seen, and I have seen my share, contain hymnals or song books for the mourners who attend. After all, there is no expectation that the attendees do anything except sit motionless, perhaps with handkerchief in hand, while the clergy person reads, prays, meditates, and commends for about twenty minutes.

But back to the "take charge" approach of the Smiths of Grinnell. If the service were to be in the church sanctuary, they showed up and invaded as if they owned the place, lock, stock, and barrel. They came with flowers in tow which they placed on altars and any other site they chose. They moved furniture around at their own discretion. They set up to conduct the ushering. The clergy person and lay leaders were treated as their guests.

Somewhere along the line at monthly clergy conclaves, some of us began to discuss the intrusive nature of the mortuary monopoly. Rev. Arvid Dixen, of St. John's Lutheran (who had become almost apoplectic about the Smiths' behavior), Rev. Michael Smith, over at First Presbyterian, and I put our collective heads together. We developed a document about appropriate conduct for morticians when approaching the sanctuary. Then, detailed complaint and constructive proposal in hand, we sat down with the Smiths.

It was what diplomats call "a frank discussion." A certain amount of dismay showed. Most of the church folk had just stepped aside. When death occurs polite behavior often increases. The Smiths had not been guilty of trying to run rough shod over appropriate protocol. Nobody had called these matters to their attention.

How can I sum up the detailed document we presented? It simply pointed out that the funeral personnel were to understand themselves as guests of the church. Whatever they proposed to place, move, hand out, etc., required the assent of the pastor and designated lay leaders. If done in that manner, they could be assured of ready and appreciative cooperation.

Did things change after that? Yes. But who knows what happened when these persnickety parsons moved on to other parishes? Reversal always hides in the wings, waiting for someone to stand up and say, "Now, wait just a minute."

## A Bell for the Belfry

A Congregational, UCC, building sits on West Maumee Street in Angola Indiana. Angola is the County Seat for Steuben County, located in the northeast corner of the state, snuggled up against Michigan to the north and Ohio to the east. In 1871 the building appeared, costing $6,000. In 1881, a steeple was added at a cost of $250.

When the church was designed, a belfry was included in the completed structure. The installation of a bell, however, escaped attention in the initial budget. In a 1910 photograph of the church no bell hung in the bell tower. There existed a rumor, no more than a whisper, that some time along the way a bell appeared, only to be followed by a fire, causing the removal of the bell. The history lay cloaked in mist.

In 1994 a bell project began to develop. We located a used bell at Brosamers Bells in Brooklyn, Michigan, costing $5,800 delivered. The bell was cast in Cincinnati, Ohio, in 1882. On a cold, blustery day a crew of nine men, led by Gary Manahan, using equipment provided by Northern Indiana Power Company, slid the bell through the belfry window and attached it to the anchored beams. They rang the bell and high-fived each other.

The bell cost the church treasury nothing. Memorial dollars honoring Florence Bowman, my mother, a member named Florence Dygert, and other donations paid for the project. A plaque memorializing the donors was placed on the wall of the Narthex.

On Sunday, December 1, 1996, the bell rang out for the first time prior to and during the 10:45 a.m. service. The Church Council agreed that a tolling of the bell would from then on initiate the call to worship for each Sunday service. The tolling? Not an announcement of the hour, but a trinitarian ringing.

I suppose my interest in church bells intensified while visiting our son, Kirk, and daughter-in-law, Edie, in Zurich in the summer of 1995. During that time the nation of Switzerland celebrated winning independence of cantons from Germany. Zurich, located on the Limmat River, celebrated by placing huge bonfires on the high hills above the city and the tolling of church bells at the appointed time. I will always remember those rumbling, echoing sounds rolling through the hills as if musical bowling balls had been loosed to roll back and forth.

A neighbor and former member of the Angola church, Barbara Doty, says the bell still rings, its B-flat tone still clear. But it's rung only occasionally. "The church is known in town as liberal," says Barbara. "More like a Unitarian Church." Not quite the faith once rung out from Jerusalem.

## Stained Glass to the Glory of God

In 1899, a church edifice emerged at 314 W. Maumee, Angola, Indiana, under the architectural hand of George Kramer. He designed forty sanctuaries in Indiana and thousands of churches in the county. His creations look like churches.

When the building went up stained glass windows came with it. Stained glass all around. In 1974, Florence P. Covell wrote a piece detailing each window, what it displayed, who donated and to whom dedicated. I remember in particular the upper section of the center window on the west side of the sanctuary: a replica of Heinrich Hofmann's "Christ in Gethsemane." One smaller window contained the letters WCTU, the Women's Christian Temperance Union. Angola, in 1899, hosted numerous saloons.

Approaching the centennial observance of the building, the February 1998 church newsletter contains a photograph of the west window with a notice below reading, "OUR WINDOWS 'IN CRISIS.' ATTEND ANNUAL MEETING!" The March 1998 newsletter, reporting on the annual meeting reads, in part, "Agreed to embark on a $30,000 funding campaign . . . to restore the centennial stained glass windows."

A Fort Wayne, Indiana, stained glass repair firm, named Lupkin, was employed. Such repair required skill and painstaking (panes taking, too) effort. They completed the job expertly and on time.

A variety of fund raising schemes ensued. Since the windows contained the abstract patterns of fish, we sold paper fish at $100 a piece as donation pledges. Amanda Syler designed scenes from the south and west windows, out of which we made beautiful note cards for sale in packets of ten. The monies appeared as the completed windows materialized, one by one. The March 1999, newsletter reads, "$31,731.73 total expenses accrued," and "$31,731.73 total monies expended. Sincerely submitted, Jim Simons."

Lots of labor donated by laity led by Cecil Fugate, with Bob Ridel, Ralph McDowell, and others, involved sanding and repairing the casements around the windows.

On Sunday, June 26, Rev. Stephen C. Gray, Conference Minister, Indiana–Kentucky United Church of Christ, spoke from the pulpit of the re-dedication of the centennial sanctuary and in celebration of the refurbished stained glass windows.

Meanwhile, we knew some articles had been placed in a cornerstone one hundred years earlier. We drilled in several likely locations. For our efforts, all we discovered was powdered stone.

But the windows, full of sacred images, shining in the morning sun, gave renewed witness to the glory of God and the efforts of the faithful.

## Weddings to Remember

It's always a bit of a risk to plan an outdoor wedding. A sudden shower may wreak havoc with the best laid plans. And what about the wedding planned for the Sunday, May 18, 1980, in Pullman, Washington?

My records show that Craig Iver Peterson and Kathleen May Cameron were scheduled to exchange vows on that fateful day, the day Mt. St. Helens blew up, scattering ash hundreds of miles to the east. The idyllic outdoor setting lay gray in two inches of dust. What to do?

So, on Monday, May 19, we drove through the dusty landscape and gathered in a fine barn, where the couple made vows and exchanged rings symbolic of their love. The barn, too, must have been dusty. That ash could filter through any crack. But they were flexible and life went on. We all wore wedding clothes and masks.

Whenever I agreed to officiate at a marriage, I always insisted on two or three pre-ceremony counseling sessions. This policy prevented me from needing to say yes to some hurry-up occasions.

Well do I remember inviting Ngoc Van Nguyen and You Eng Taing to my office for marriage counseling. I expected just the twosome. In my naiveté, I did not realize the families of the couple would come as well.

This was an arranged marriage. The couple had never met. What's more, as they sat in the church office she would not look at him, since that also lay outside the proper custom.

I found myself wanting to ask a question I often asked, "Do you love him?" and "Do you love her?" I did not ask. I realized there could be no real answer. The question I did not ask, "Do you trust your parents?" All went well at the wedding. Our older daughter, Moira, served as bridesmaid and our younger daughter, Rachel, sang. There followed a reception, including a Cambodian dinner with several courses. All in all it was a wonderful occasion.

Then there was the outdoor wedding at Hidden Lake Gardens, a beautiful spot. I do not seem to have a record of the couple's names, which is just as well. Let me set the scene: The couple and I were to meet on a platform at the lower end of the pond. So the groom and I found our way to said spot. The music began, something country, played from a pickup truck parked along the pond's edge. Then the bride emerged out of trees at the far end of the pond. Dressed in flouncy white she minced her way toward us along the pond's edge, precariously, her high heels sinking in the mud. How shall I say it politely? She was not petite. The guitar music sounded and on she advanced toward us. It was not Lohengrin or Purcell. Maybe Garth Brooks. Miraculously having escaped plunging into the pond, she arrived at the platform.

With renewed assurance, I began to present the service. A serious moment? Not for them. At each point, he laughed and she joined in. Not mocking. More nervousness, I guess. But disconcerting, to say the least. I remember praying to myself, "O Lord, how did I get myself into this?"

I never saw them again. I hope they lived together happily ever after.

## A Roof for the Lord's House

In the latter half of 2005 I delivered a brief interim ministry to the Congregational Church at Morenci, Michigan. After the 8:30 a.m. service in Morenci, we began driving across the state line, a one-half hour distance, to Wauseon, Ohio, where the Congregational United Church of Christ worshiped at 11:00 a.m. About that time Rev. William Smith concluded his seven year ministry there.

The City of Wauseon, located west of Toledo, in the heart of Fulton County, boasts prime farmland for corn and soy beans. The church, when I encountered it, had fallen to low ebb in numbers and financial strength. A few stalwarts prayed and worked for a brighter future.

After I indicated interest in serving the Wauseon congregation on an interim basis, two lay leaders, Lawrence McClarren and his son-in-law, Rex Oyer, stopped by my bookstore, The Bookery, in Adrian, Michigan.

## The Parish Church Building

Both grain farmers, I guess they were checking if I were worth harvesting. On January 8, 2006, the congregation and I held our first service together.

The handsome brick building at the corner of Clinton and Elm, in downtown Wauseon, was prone to baptism—water rising in the basement and showers, not necessarily of blessing, penetrating the fifty-year-old roof.

Soon we began a financial campaign to put a new roof on the sanctuary and to repair the basement axillary rooms. The effort went well. On November 7, 2007, Bill Kerr, Rex Oyer, and Lawrence McClarren handed the contractor, Dave Birt of Lima, Ohio, the final check of $51,000. The project also included gutters, down spouting, plexiglas protection of stained-glass windows, and tuck pointing. We received donations from forty members and friends of the church, plus sizable gifts from Jewel Kintzinger of Grinnell, Iowa (former parishioner), and the Bethel Church of Manchester, Michigan, where I had been Interim Minister.

The edifice effort seems to have strengthened the backbone of the congregation. Other aspects of church life and work brightened. The congregation, begun in 1862, celebrated its 150th Anniversary on June 24, 2012, with a renewed sense of faith and hope.

On August 24, 2008, on the verge of our move to California, the congregation held a "Goodbye Party" for Dianne and me. A pictorial folder presented, included lots of pleasant words, including those from the pillars of the congregation, Lawrence and Irene McClarren, saying, "You both gave us so much, renewed our hopes physically and spiritually, truly leaving your imprints on our hearts."

That two-and-one-half years with the fine people of the Wauseon church seem to have been attended by the Spirit of God, enabling our common endeavors. William Kerr, whose family has deep roots in the church, is now the pastor.

### Fire!

Entering any new ministry surprises await. That proved true in Wauseon, Ohio, the County Seat of farmland rich Fulton County.

I discovered that just about the time I prepared to make the most salient point of the morning message the railway freight express, on the way through Wauseon, headed for Toledo, would come screaming through town. The tracks lay only a block away. Thoughts tended to wander.

Then, to my dismay, this congregation owned only a silly millimeter of land outside the south wall of the church building. To make matters worse, the neighbor had a grudge against the church and prohibited a ladder going up on his property in order to make needed church repairs. When we came to put on a new roof we had to go to court to gain permission and pay him a right-of-way fee.

And then there was the discovery, on the verge of performing my first Ohio wedding, that I needed a certificate from the Secretary of State's Office in Columbus, Ohio, in order to make me a legal officiant. How out of the ordinary. A new one on me.

Then came the big surprise. On Saturday, April 14, 2007, one-fourth of the business district of downtown Wauseon burned down. The fire started in the Doc Holiday Restaurant some time in the night. The stores running north on Fulton Street (the main drag) to Elm and then west on Elm for half a block, there existing no firewall between them, one after another caught fire. Fire brigades from town and the surrounding regions descended on the scene. Extra water was trucked in. Flames! Streams of water! Pandemonium!

The church building of Congregational United Church of Christ had stood at the corner of Elm and Clinton since 1904. Now the downtown fire licked its way to a narrow alley between a photography store and the east wall of the church.

Bill Kerr, a member, had called me earlier (4:00 a.m.) to say, "Dave, you'd better come down. The downtown's on fire. The church is in danger." As I drove the thirty miles south from Adrian, Michigan, I could see the smoke rising against the morning sky.

When I arrived, I found a place to stand midst the melee in a parking lot across Elm Street from the church. Several times I shouted to a man with a fire hose, "Throw more water on the church roof!" Indeed, sparks flew and smoke billowed toward the church. How fortunate that in 2006 we had put on a new roof and new plexiglas coverings on the stained-glass windows. I doubt the fifty-year-old roof would have withstood the sparks or the intense water streams. Either fire or significant water damage! As it was, the church insurance covered the cleaning of the interior from the infiltration of smoke.

The owner of the above-named restaurant was indicted for arson. He was not convicted. Up and down the street folk doubted his exoneration, since he had previously had a business that was not doing well, burn down.

Meanwhile, under a renewal city/business plan new and stronger structures soon emerged.

The church building—"some through the water, some through fire, all through the blood"—stands handsomely at Clinton and Elm—stalwart people inside still involved in witness and service in Christ's name.

## A Church Called Bethel

Bethel Church, Manchester, Michigan, traces its heritage to German farmers who settled in the mid–eighteen hundreds. With Ann Arbor, home of the University of Michigan, twenty minutes away, diversity threatens to intrude, but the German heritage persists, deeply rooted. Bethel's *kirche* held German services as late as the 1950s.

In January 2003, Rev. Richard Hardy moved to Berea, Ohio. I had begun to minister as an interim Interim. At the February 16 Church Board meeting four Interim candidates, two men and two women, emerged for consideration. The board agreed to interview each of them.

On March 3, Pat Laberdee approached me inquiring about my willingness, if asked, to become Interim Minister. I replied, "I am not interested in throwing my hat in the ring and going through some formal interview process along with other candidates . . . You know me already."

The May issue of "Bethel Newsletter" noted that I had been in the pulpit since early February and that the Church Board had unanimously asked me to become Interim Minister. Larry Guenther, President, announced this on Palm/Passion Sunday, April 13. While no overt search on my part preceded these events, I felt pleased to be on hand. No longer was I just interim Interim.

I hit the ground running at Bethel. Running to keep up. The lay leadership led activity, not waiting on clergy signals. Women as well as men. In fact, I found myself encouraging the men to catch up.

Bethel! What a name! Long ago, while journeying, Jacob came to a certain place. Night was falling, and so selecting a stone for a pillow, he settled down to sleep. And he dreamed of messengers of God descending to and ascending from that place. And he heard the Lord say that even as his father Abraham had known divine guidance, so he also would be led.

When Jacob awoke, he said, "Surely the Lord is in this place, and I did not know it . . . How awesome is this place! This is none other than the house of God. This is the gate of heaven" (See Gen 28:10-17).

In Hebrew he said, *Beth-El,* which translated means House of God.

Bethel. As a church member, Bonnie Mitchell once said, "Picturesque, among the pines, set on a hilltop in the rolling countryside." On a road named for it, a house of God.

# The People of the Parish

"The Communion of Saints" . . . and—within it—an eternal life.

DAG HAMMARSKJÖLD, *Markings*[1]

---

1. Hammarskjöld, *Markings*, 84.

## The Gathering

DURING THE 1971–1982 PERIOD of ministry in Pullman, Washington, I served a congregation whose building stood adjacent to the WSU campus. From the outset we reached out an invitation to university students.

Beginning on Sunday, October 6, 1974, we hosted a group of students and sought to integrate them into the life of the church. A few of these were married couples; most of the group came as individuals. We called the assemblage The Gathering.

We met regularly during the school year in the Fireside Room of the church. Our agenda? Build a group capable of offering mutual concern. Offer Bible study. Create activities designed to engender interaction. Provide opportunities for service in the congregation and beyond. Oh yes, and eat, eat, eat.

We usually enjoyed a group of a dozen or so. They were a lively bunch. Being not too long in the tooth at the time—late twenties and early thirties—I felt able not only to offer leadership but also to interact closely with them. Numerous times we invited The Gathering to our house for backyard croquet under the lights and eats, eats, eats.

The Washington/N. Idaho Conference, UCC, maintained a beautiful, accommodating retreat center on Lake Coeur d'Alene. On several occasions The Gathering retreated to that facility as a getaway from the pressures of campus life and to further develop a spirit of Christian community.

On November 29, 1981, the first Sunday in Advent, the focus of the morning worship centered on the Book of Revelation, a text appropriate for Advent. Eleven members of The Gathering presented a verbal and visual drama I had written for the occasion.

The drama presented, "The Apocalypse," in totality, moving from prologue through seven acts to the epilogue. Members of The Gathering spoke as narrator, heralding angel, John, and other entities such as "the seven churches." The drama featured interspersed recorded music fitting the mood and hymns sung by the congregation.

A typical comment following the service: "The young people performed well but I still don't understand Revelation." Perhaps. But Revelation is not so much to be comprehended as experienced in something of the same way one encounters a magnificent water fall.

Never again in my ministry would I have a college group of this nature. I remember that November service as much for the enthusiastic participation of The Gathering as for the content of the drama.

## Dreaming of a Greens Christmas

A couple of weeks before Christmas, on a Saturday morning, members and friends in the parish would gather at the church, dressed in outdoor clothing. Clambering into our vehicles we headed east for the forests, there to cut trees and greenery for church and home. Then, loaded with the conifers, we returned to the church, there to decorate Sanctuary, Narthex, and classrooms for the season. All this took place with jolly moods over coffee, hot chocolate and donuts.

This all took place in Pullman, a burg in eastern Washington, once known as Three Forks, but renamed Pullman when the city fathers believed the railway magnate, George Pullman, would send a generous reward for such naming—a fortune that never arrived. Pullman, known best as the location of WSU (known on the west side of the state as "the Party School" but known to WSU loyalists for its fine traditions in broadcast communication and agricultural sciences), lies just to the west of the Idaho state line and its dense northern forests. Each year the Idaho Forest Service would mark off treed areas with yellow streamers. There folk from the region could feel free to cut and load up a couple of trees to decorate for the season.

One remembers these occasions for their sheer fun, the building of community within the parish and the kick-off of celebrating the birth of Jesus.

## Christmas Eve in Pullman

It's of interest how some events have a settled niche in our memories, while other occasions of a parallel ilk retain no place on our historical screen.

Christmas Eve in Pullman, Washington. My thoughts rush back; images and sounds flood together.

We always held one service only. The pews would fill. A time for creative liturgies, a healthy mix of scripture, carols, poetry, and a final "Silent Night" with candles held around the periphery of the sanctuary.

I never offered a traditional pulpit word. Rather I would tell a fictional story, such as R. M. Alden's, "Why the Chimes Rang," or "The Fourth Wiseman," from Henry Van Dyke.

We never included Holy Communion. Since the pews would fill up with folk we had never seen before and likely would never see again, the idea of partaking in communion with those who shared a common reverence for the occasion seemed out the window. Some will argue this places too high a fence around the table. I would simply argue that, "This is my body," and, "This is my blood," ought to have more import than the bottle of beer an hour later.

A number of times students and friends from the adjacent WSU campus occupied the front rows. Occasionally they were a bit noisy. That was okay. We were pleased to welcome them for this celebration of the night of all nights.

Left over from my predecessor, Rev. Theodore Edquist, came the poem for the evening. Most years we read it toward the end of the service. Titled, "Christmas Always Comes at Night," a portion of it reads as follows:

> Christmas always comes at night
> When men grope blindly for a light.
> Christmas could not come by day,
> That is not God's or nature's way!
> Can Wise Men see a star at noon?
> Can Shepherds hear the Angels' tune
> When the sun is bright?
>
> Death on the Cross will come at eve
> When weary daylight takes its leave—
> And Resurrection fits the dawn
> When patterns for the new days are drawn.

> But Christmas comes in deepest dark—
> Through black despair men see a spark
> Embattled with the night!
>
> So, Christmas always comes at night
> When men are hungriest for light!
> Can Wise Men see a star at noon?
> Can Shepherds hear the Angels' tune
> When sun is bright?
> Christmas comes in deepest dark
> When in despair man sees a spark
> Conquering the night![2]

As I said, the congregation having circled the sanctuary, leaving an offering at the Chancel steps on the way, received the light from the Christ Candle, borne to them by the acolytes. Then "Stille Nacht." We tried to end at midnight. Then rang chimes from the organ for Christmas Day.

I would then offer a Christmas Prayer. In 1981, my penultimate Christmas in Pullman, the prayer arose as follows:

> O Thou, who over time has made yourself known in sacramental moments, fleeting dreams, and prophetic words, we rejoice that you have revealed yourself in the Child born in the manger and in our lives through faith.
>
> We give thanks that we have been included in the knowledge of this joy. And we pray we may not grow *blasé* or immune to the surprise of this good news. Rather may we sense again in the moment and in this season the wonder of it all, the unfathomable mystery, that with awe and reverence we too may bow and own this expression of yourself as our Savior and our Lord.
>
> With all others of good will we pray that peace and justice will descend on troubled places because folk stop and hear the song, "Peace on earth, good will to all people."

And the benediction:

> Now the peace of God which comes in the One born among us, whose Spirit neither leaves us or forsakes us, go with you where you play, travel and work, giving you a joy the world can never give. Amen.

---

2. Elmer, *World in Ferment*, 32–33.

Then, at the door, coats and scarves in place, we would wish each other, "Merry Christmas," and walk out midst the gently falling snow. The street lights lighted the night scape. All was calm. All was bright. All was right. I remember it as if it were yesterday. In eternal time it was not even that long ago.

## An Unbidden Tear

During the 1971–1982 period, when in ministry in Pullman, Washington, we were fortunate to have an African-American couple, William and Gaston Moseley, as members of the congregation. They brought style, dignity and a jovial spirit to any occasion.

Frequently Mr. Mosely read the Old Testament lesson and/or the Epistle in the Sunday morning service. He deemed it his responsibility not only to read the sacred text but to give educated interpretive remarks prior to the reading. Though he was well prepared, sometimes the length of his preface led us in silence to question, "When is he going to get to the text?"

This couple of retirement age moved to Pullman to be close to their son, David, and his spouse, Sonja, along with their grandchildren, Sarah and Tinka. The local university, WSU, employed David in some capacity.

On one occasion I paid a pastoral visit to Bill and Gaston's home. Gaston and I took seats in the living room to talk, absent Bill. I retain no memory of the subject of conversation, but I could take you to the exact point where she and I sat in the room. Then the memorable part of the occasion took place.

As we talked I began to weep. Nothing from the conversation itself evoked the tears. Wiping my eyes with a handkerchief, I simply said to Gaston, "I'm weeping for all the past." "I know," she said, and fell silent.

There we sat in that well-appointed living room. Comfortable. No threats about. No slave master at the door calling her to duty. She, a graduate of Spelman College in Atlanta, Georgia, holding an MA in social work. Educated. Insightful. A faithful follower of Christ. She the daughter of someone who caught hold of the chariot when it swung low. She the offspring of someone who rode the "underground railroad" or urgently wished they could. She, a part of the legacy who followed the "drinking gourd" northward.

Maybe for a moment I was back in my childhood church, where my father, Rev. Charles W. Bowman, had invited the Lacey Colored Trio to hold revival services in the Taylorville Church of the Nazarene in central Illinois. My father, whose brothers would sit in their Chicago living rooms, smoking long cigars and telling racist jokes. My father, not better than those two, but more instructed and inspired by the Man of Nazareth. Miss Woodson stood up and began to sing:

> Tell me, how did you feel
> When you come out the wilderness,
> Come out the wilderness,
> Come out the wilderness,
> Leanin' on the Lord?[3]

Perhaps unconsciously in retrospect, I saw my father wipe a tear from his eye. An unbidden tear. A tear left over from all those dark, nasty slave ships, a tear from all those beastly hot cotton fields, a tear from all those non–consensual sexual encounters between slave owner and serf, a tear for those families separated when a child, torn from parents' arms, rode off in a wagon to another plantation, a tear for all "the stony roads they trod."

I wept. Mrs. Moseley, across the room, looked up. She said, "I understand." My father's tears. My own. All of ours.

## That You May Be Healed

The passage in The Letter of James reads, "Are any among us sick? They should call for the elders of the church and have them pray over them, anointing them with oil in the name of the Lord. The prayer of faith will save the sick and the Lord will raise them up" (Jas 5:14-15a).

My brief commentary on that passage is as follows: If the congregation has more than the historic two or three, then count on it, someone is sick . . . Calling for "the elders" may mislead these days, given the aging of the church. "Summon the presbyters" (New American Bible) is more literal, but that too may confuse those who do not use that term regularly. So let us just say, Ask "the saints" to gather round, especially those who know the person and may already have been offering intercessory prayer on behalf of the ill person . . . And one more necessary comment is in order: Surely

---

3. Anon., *United Methodist*, 416.

the assurance that the sick one will be healed and raised up rings false. We may say, "It will do no harm." We may also say, "It may help in the healing process." Surely James, based on vast experience, should have said no more.

Only twice in my ministry have I put oil on the forehead of an ill person and offered a prayer for healing. (Well, maybe I did so more often but that is the extent of my memory. After all, even St. Paul could not remember exactly how many times he baptized [1 Cor 1:15].) Once in the chapel beside the church in Angola, Indiana, when the gentleman and myself were alone. The other time I will speak of more in detail.

The issue was cancer. The woman so diagnosed and under medical treatment, was a faithful member of the parish, along with her husband and two sons. I am not sure whether she made the suggestion or if I brought the possibility to her attention. Anyway, at the appointed time, she, along with family and church friends, gathered at the altar in the sanctuary. I applied oil and prayed. We all prayed. I believe all of us felt it had been a helpful, even efficacious, occasion.

In my theological perspective, the Spirit of God is always at work for our general welfare. As the psalmist says, "No good thing does the Lord withhold from those who walk uprightly" (Ps 84:11b). Certain scriptural teachings lie outside my framework of interpretation such as, "Therefore, let those who suffer in accordance with God's will entrust themselves to a faithful creator, while continuing to do good" (1 Pet 4:19). Empirical evidence supports the biblical teaching that unbelief hinders the healing influence of God. As the evangelist reports, "And he (Jesus) did not do many deeds of power there (Nazareth) because of their unbelief" (Matt 13:58). The will of God for our wellness accompanies the natural decay of aging, which does not seem to exist in contradiction to the divine will, since we are dust and to dust we return (See Eccl 3:20). I believe, too, that the divine will struggles immensely to exert wholesome influence in the world while contested by an oppositional power. It is this mystery the apostle speaks of when he refers to the wrestling match of God and the would-be faithful "not against enemies of blood and flesh, but against rulers, against the authorities, against the cosmic powers of this present darkness, against the spiritual forces of evil in the heavenly places" (Eph 6:12).

In some churches these days people in the pews may be invited forward, usually prior to the observance of Holy Communion, to receive the imposition of oil and prayer for healing. I have no objection, but it seems to me a bit casual. And why should the clergy person be the only one who prays? I believe the occasion spoken of in the Epistle of James ought to be more like what people in AA call "an intervention." This includes the presence of the important persons in one's life. The illness is confronted, and, in this case, prayers arise. The positive psychosomatic effect of such times may be considerable. Who knows how much "unbelief" and "cosmic powers" might be scattered.

On reflection, perhaps I ought to have engaged in such ministry more often. It is no excuse, but nowhere in my process of education toward ministry was I encouraged in this direction, neither in evangelical or mainline Protestant circles. That is just an observation, not an excuse.

## Adult Fare

Over time I have contended for the role of adult education in the local church.

Too many sincere members labor along on the education they received in Sunday School. For example, occasions when the Noah and the flood story came across to children as a literal happening, presented on the basis of children's fascination with animals. At what point, other than secular education, do Christian laity find intellectual equipment to find meaning in such stories beyond the childlike considerations?

It was the ethicist, James Gustafson, who said that among other elements the church is to be "a community of moral discourse." Exactly. Not in a top down dogmatic fashion, but in a dialogue setting, the issues of the time require to be run through the sieve of the faith tradition.

At Park Church, Grand Rapids, Michigan, in addition to focus on youth ministry, I had the opportunity to participate in just such a discourse. Naming a few of these focus events will indicate their outward looking nature:

- *The Biological Time Bomb*, by Gordon Rattray Taylor–A review of the book by a biology professor, a Jewish rabbi, a physician and a Catholic priest.
- "Doing Grand Rapids"—Rev. Stephen Vesbit and I led the participants into a downtown bar, next to the rapids of the Grand River, and a number of other locations, "to get the feel and pulse" of the city and then to take time to reflect on what we had experienced.

- "The Christian Use of Power"—A consideration of urgent matters such as disarmament, the Vietnam conflict, the Selective Service System, all in the midst of those turbulent late 1960s time.
- "The New Morality"—A discussion of the debate especially raised by Joseph Fletcher's *Situation Ethics*. A college professor, an Episcopal priest, and I offered thoughts for discussion.

"Draft Information Forum"—Presentations from American Friends Service Committee, Army Recruitment Service, a local Draft Board and the Draft Information Center. The date: March 11, 1970. The air was electric.

That's just a sample of what went down over the three-year period, 1968–1971. We could not be accused of hiding out in the sanctuary. Neither would a criticism of "presenting only one side" have held water.

Never later in various other parishes did we have the resources or the available lay and clergy leadership to offer such an array of adult opportunities. In other sites I often wished an ecumenical focus around themes might develop. Seldom did such chances occur. The tendency for parishes and their clergy to hide out in their own bailiwicks prevailed.

## A Moment in Time

Coiled like a rattler, State Highway 52 winds down from Chelsea to Manchester, Michigan. Near the village the road plunges downward to the right, running in front of a precipitous property then owned by Mark and Betty Muszynski.

Betty, beloved wife, attentive mother, busied herself that morning with the details of a yard sale. The date: July 11, 2003.

What first claimed Betty's attention? A glint in the morning mist? The sound of tires crunching grass? An old orange pick-up hurtled toward her. No brakes were applied. There was no time to leap aside. The vehicle, having left the road, hit her once, knocking her many yards, then rumbled on, running over her. Later at University of Michigan Hospital the family gathered and waited. Distressed, agitated, prayerful.

Betty, faithful Christian woman, fought for her life. "The rain," as Jesus once put it, "falls on the just and the unjust" (Matt 5:45).

Betty's recovery? Noting short of amazing. Dare we say miraculous. Young, strong, and lithe of limb. ("No mere slip of a woman," we might say.) This stood her in good stead. But the main human recovery factors were skillful rescue and medical personnel, supportive family and church, and constructive attitude. Betty, and Mark too, displayed, to a remarkable degree, lack of anger. Almost devoid of "why me!" Instead, she trusted in God and willed to get well.

She did.

On Sunday, October 12, 2003, Betty and family were back at Bethel Church. Second row on the lectern side. The minister, yours truly, spoke on, "God Works in All Events." He quoted from Rev. Konow, then pastor at Zion Lutheran Church, Chelsea: "We serve God who is with us in life and in death. We serve a God who, though the seasons of life may change, remains unchanging. And we serve a God who in the midst of our brokenness provides healing and wholeness."

Thanks be to God!

## They Called It Cadre

A perennial issue: How does faith relate to and influence contemporary life? Conscious of new forms of the church, such as Taize in France and Iona in Scotland, in 1962 the Church Federation of Greater Chicago organized "The Ecumenical Institute (EI)." They invited Dr. Joseph Wesley Matthews from Dallas, Texas, to become Dean. Seven families moved to the area on Chicago's west side, known as 5th City. The group engaged in a commune lifestyle with focus on worship, study, and service. By 1968, according to Wikipedia, the Chicago group numbered over one hundred people. By 1974 the membership grew to 1,500 working in over one hundred offices in twenty nations.

When I came to Park Church, in Grand Rapids, Michigan, the influence of EI could be felt. Under the leadership of Rev. Roger "Derry" Henneman, a "cadre" of members existed for study and service. Part of my job description called for leadership of this body. Without much awareness of the background of the EI, I plunged into the challenge of "cadre."

Our agenda? Developed by consensus we (a) surveyed a large number of young adults in Grand Rapids as to their feelings toward the organized church, out of which grew a position paper; (b) concluded an internal survey about Cadre's continuing plans; (c) studied scripture; (d) took retreats to study and build community; and (e) developed and distributed among the church members a "Statement of Theological Perspective at the Time of the 1968 National Election."

## Parish, the Thought

The theological perspective statement grew out of the candidacy for President of Governor George Wallace. It was based on the format of The Theological Declaration of Barmen expressed by the Confessional Churches in 1934 as a protest of the policies of the Reich Government of Germany. The pattern was (a) a Bible verse; (b) a theological proposition; and (c) an application of the principle to the current scent.

This statement appeared in the October 30, 1968, edition of the weekly "Park Congregationalist." It read as follows:

> The members of Cadre, speaking only for themselves, in the attempt to apply the teachings of the Christian faith to our particular hour in history, present the following statement of conviction concerning the approaching national election and the issues which have been raised.
>
> FEAR OR LOVE
>
> *"Perfect love casts out fear"* (1 John 4:18).
>
> *"Welcome one another therefore, as Christ as welcomed you, for the glory of God* (Rom 15:7).
>
> All men of good will desire to live together in harmony and understanding. Christians are required by their Lord to be at peace with their neighbors.
>
> **Fear is a human condition, but we oppose those who attempt to gain political favor by FEEDING these several fears:**
>
> > loss of educational advantage
> > loss of hard-earned property
> > loss of job security
> > loss of local autonomy
>
> LAW AND JUSTICE
>
> *"He has showed you, O man, what is good; and what does the Lord require of you but to do justice, and to love kindness, and to walk humbly with your God?"* (Mic 6:8).
>
> Most of us do not adequately understand the level of suffering which underlies much of the lawlessness in our land. In the presence of inequities, the undue emphasis on "Law and Order," without mercy, is not Christian.

The repetition of the phrase, "Law and Order," has tended to blur the issues in this election year. Christians ought NOT to support those who have talked only of law and order without offering remedies for social ills.

## WAR OR PEACE

*"Through the tender mercy of our God . . . the day shall dawn upon us from on high to give light to those who sit in darkness and in the shadow of death, to guide our feet into the way of peace"* (Luke 1:78–79).

Christians regard war as a plague upon mankind. We support and encourage current efforts toward peace in Paris and elsewhere.

**Vietnam is an ugly war. Therefore, we oppose those who, under present circumstances, favor expansion of military hostilities.**

## SUPPORT AND DISSENT

*"Render therefore to Caesar the things that are Caesar's, and to God the things that are God's"* (Matt 22:21).

Christians have often exercised freedom of conscience in making decisions. Therefore, we recognize and support the right of members of a free society to dissent against established authorities in matters pertaining to moral judgment.

**When active dissent takes the form of violence, endangering the lives and infringing upon the rights of others, Christians should actively oppose it. But we oppose those who would suppress legitimate dissent within our society.**

## PEOPLE

*"From one ancestor he made all nations to inhabit the earth . . . "* (Acts 17:26a).

It is the ancient belief of the Church that all men, regardless of apparent differences, are the "common offspring" of the One True God. It is this divine image in man, as well as our common humanity, which binds us together in the movement toward brotherhood in this time of crisis.[4]

---

4. The often exclusive reference to the male gender, when meaning to all humanity, had not been much questioned in 1968.

> Christians ought then to renounce publicly anyone who openly favors the separation of peoples, particularly in the vital areas of education, housing, and labor.
>
> *"Seek the welfare of the city where I have sent you into exile, and pray to the Lord on its behalf, for in its welfare you will find your welfare"* (Jer 29:7).

This last proposition, concerning segregation, applied most directly to Governor Wallace. By that November election he had garnered a significant following in Michigan.

When it came time to baptize our second child, Moira Dawn, we chose not to hold the service in the sanctuary in the midst of the whole congregation. Rather, we invited members of Cadre and spouses to attend a service in the alternate worship area of the church, Thompson Chapel. This seemed to us, at the time, a more intimate expression and authentic of Christian community.

## Sibling Love

In the life of Bethel Church, Manchester, Michigan, celebration of the family takes place often. The sacred bond between a man and a woman before God, with the fruit of their love in birth, finds constant focus. Newcomers find ready welcome, but the extended family characterizes the Bethel tradition. True to say, one ought never bad mouth another member, not only for good Christian reasons, but because the reference may be to a cousin or an uncle.

One of the traditions at Bethel is as follows: On a given Sunday morning, often when a baby in the congregation first appears in worship, a rose is placed on the altar table. The minister then takes the rose from the altar table and in person delivers it to the parent or parents.

So it was on Sunday, June 8, 2003, I approached Will and Amy Riley, who in pride held their second child, their first-born boy, Liam. The congregation applauded. Then something memorable happened.

It seemed that Lauren, Liam's sister, wanted to speak into the microphone. She was three years old at the time. In a clearly audible, steady voice she said, "I just want to say I love my brother very much!" That's an exact quote.

Everyone in the room felt in that moment they had been to church. A celebration of God's gift of family. Scarcely could an anthem, a prayer, or a pulpit word have said more, or said it better.

Out of the mouths of babes, indeed!

## Confirming One's Baptism

Infant baptism is practiced in the UCC tradition. I always insisted that this event take place in the midst of the congregation. If it were to be a home occasion, then a couple of Deacons or other members were invited. It is an act of the church.

Writing this reminds me of an unusual request arising at the UCC in Wauseon, Ohio, where in 2007 to 2008 I served as Interim Minister. My Christian Church/Disciples colleague, a block away, came to me saying, "I have three couples who wish to have their infants baptized. But we Disciples only do believers baptism. Would you come to my church and baptize these children but not in our public worship?" I replied, "I would be pleased to do that under two conditions. One, I have a chance to speak with the parents about the meanings of infant baptism, and two, that adult members of your church who are comfortable with this event, attend." And so it happened just like that.

In churches I served we nearly always had a year-long confirmation class usually with young people of the eighth or ninth grade level. In the tradition, many young people went through catechetical memorization of certain materials, such as parts of The Heidelberg Catechism. I sought to use resources about the Bible and theology that connected more closely with the lived experience of the youth.

In many churches the tradition views confirmation training as a greased pole to confirmation. I always insisted that to confirm one's baptism included a personal sense of being led by God's Spirit into such an affirmation. With that in mind I encouraged the young people, now on the verge of adulthood, to resist the threefold pressures of family, church, and tradition.

In most classes I conducted over the years, the young people moved on to Confirmation Day. It was not for me, the pastor, to know how much of the vows taken represented personal conviction or what just amounted to doing what was expected.

One year, in a church where the expectation to be confirmed ran high, a young man, named George, said, "I'm just not ready to take that step." I made sure I let the parents know that I affirmed his delay on the basis of conscience just as much as I affirmed the dozen or so who made vows and received first communion on Confirmation Sunday.

I have no idea where George is today. I hope he is a man of faith and active in the church. I recall clearly those who have said to me, "I was so pressured as a young person I've never been back," and others who have said to me earnestly, "I'm so glad I was led into confirmation. In the end it brought me back to faith and the life of the church."

I always valued the opportunity to teach the faith and the chance to nurture young lives. Always, too, with a sense of fear and trembling.

## A Blessing from Kenya

Sometimes of a morning the parish minister may not be quite sure about the priority for the day. There's always the Sunday message to prepare and pastoral visitations await. Administrative concerns lie in wait on the church office desk. But what new call does the day bring?

While minister at First Congregational, Angola, Indiana, we worked closely with Darrel Schoen, Director of International Services at nearby Tri-State University (now known as Trine University). Our church building hosted the annual international students' Thanksgiving Dinner.

One morning I took notice of the fact that Mr. Schoen kept putting out a notice that a new faculty member needed housing. I responded.

This response occasioned a first and mutually significant meeting. Dr. Sammy Tumuti, come to the university to teach psychology, hailed from Kenya where he gave lay leadership among Presbyterians. We found housing for him.

Dr. Tumuti, a well-spoken and engaging man, entered into the active life of our church. At various times he gave the Sunday homily. He taught in our Church School. For a time he served as Sexton. Our congregation, with his leadership, made contributions to the Kenya Christian School.

We became aware that Dr. Tumuti came to the United States not only to further his own learning (an MA at Washington University, St. Louis, and a PhD at Southern Illinois University, Carbondale, Illinois), but also to enhance the education of Abraham and Joshua, his stalwart sons.

As our relationship deepened we were able to assist Abraham (Abe Thuku) and Joshua (Josh Wachirah) in their higher education plans. Through our UCC contacts we helped Abraham enter Elmhurst College, where he earned his degree. Later our Church Council, at my request, became the guarantor for a college loan, enabling Joshua to attend Knox College. He graduated there and paid off his college loan on time.

We learned, too, of Dr. Dinah Wargui Tumuti Wachira, Sammy's's spouse, who continued to teach at Kenyatta University in Nairobi. She was alone, without husband and sons, during a period in 1998 when the university closed because of political turmoil and violence. In late 1998 Dinah, in London for a conference, sought a visa to visit her family in Angola, Indiana. The United States Department of Immigration would not grant it, fearing she would overstay her allotted time. We exhausted numerous angles, but to no avail. Finally, we turned to Paul Oakes, a member of the church, who had a personal relationship with veteran Senator, Richard Lugar. Following Paul's appeal, the senator broke through the bureaucratic snafu. Dinah arrived for a joyful Christmas visit.

Having completed his central objective—the enhancement of his sons' education—Sammy returned to Kenya and to Dinah. He became Director of the Wellness Center at Kenyatta University where Dinah had continued as Director of Community Outreach. He resumed his lay leadership role in the Presbyterian Church of East Africa, the Kakawa Sukari Church in Sukari Parish. On February 19, 2012, the parish held a retirement service for their elder, Dr. Sammy Timuti. He has since become one of the saints who from their labors rest.

Both Abraham and Joshua have returned to Kenya, where at last report Abraham is running a school in conjunction with a team in Chicago and Joshua is a lecturer at Kenyata University, working on his PhD.

Dr. Sammy Tumuti, smart, disciplined, courageous. One of the saints along the way. When reaching out to him, the parish minister, on that day, had his priorities right

## When Helga Prayed

Bethel Church, and its environs, constitutes something of a sociological phenomenon. Germans emigrated to the Ann Arbor area in the 1840s, cut some trees, removed some rock, and hitched the horses to the plow. Not that Bethel is the only location the "melting pot" failed to materialize, but in how many congregations in mobile USA do you hear a confirmand announce, "I'm the seventh generation in this congregation." So, the Germanic roots probed deeply. Families were fairly large and close-knit; children tended to set up households down the road or around the corner.

The historical marker in front of the church reads, in part, "German services were held here until 1955." The German tradition flowed on but the Germanic tongue disappeared. Who now can utter a *"Guten Morgen"* or an *"Auf Wiedersehen"* ? Scarcely anyone.

But one Sunday morning Helga Raab agreed to offer The Lord's Prayer in German. Helga, nearing the end of her earthly days, embodied that Evangelical and Reformed German faith tradition. Her father, F. C. Lueckhoff, had served for nineteen years as Superintendent of the German Protestant Home for Orphans and Old People in Detroit, Michigan. Prior to that office he had served in parish ministry.

When the time came, from her pew, without microphone, she prayed. A special silence fell throughout the sanctuary. Helga prayed:

> *Vater unser im Himmel*
> *geheiligt werde dein Name;*
> *dein Reich komme;*
> *dein Wille geschehe,*
> *wie im Himmel so auf Erden.*
> *Unser tägliches Brot gib uns heute.*
> *Und vergib uns unsere Schuld,*
> *wie auch wir vergeben unsern Schuldigern;*
> *und führe uns nicht in Versuchung,*
> *sondern erlöse uns von dem Bösen.*
> *Denn dein ist das Reich und die Kraft*
> *und die Herrlichkeit in Ewigkeit.*
> *Amen.*

The saints in the adjoining cemetery listened hard. The walls of the "old stone church" heard familiar syllables. Some sitting in the pews heard their parents and grandparents pray again. Surely heaven heard.

# Bibliography

Anonymous. *The United Methodist Hymnal*. Nashville: Abingdon, 1989.

Barth, Karl. *The Word of God and the Word of Man*. Translated by Douglas Horton, London: Hodder and Stoughton, 1928.

Berrigan, Daniel. "Christians in a War Making State." In *Testimony: The Word Made Fresh*. UK: Orbis, 1968.

———. *Love, Love at the End: Parables, Prayers and Meditations*. New York: Macmillan, 1968.

Buechner, Frederich. *Telling Secrets: A Memoir*. New York: Harper Collins, 2009.

———. *Telling the Truth: The Gospel as Tragedy, Comedy and Fairy Tale*. New York: Harper & Row, 1977.

Chase, Loring D. *Words of Faith*. Boston: United Church, 1968.

Deitz, Purd E. "We Would Be Building." In *The New Century Hymnal*. Cleveland: Pilgrim, 1995.

Douglass, James W. *The Nonviolent Coming of God*. Maryknoll: Orbis, 1993.

Elmer, Franklin D. "Christmas Always Comes at Night." In *World in Ferment*. South Bristol: Sky Tide, 1981.

Gearhart, Sally and William Johnson. *Loving Women/Loving Men: Gay Liberation and the Church*. San Francisco: Glide, 1974.

Hammarskjöld, Dag. *Markings*. London: Faber and Faber, 1964.

Hatfield, Mark. *Between a Rock and a Hard Place*. Waco: Word, 1976.

Hazelton, Roger. *Christ and Ourselves: A Clue to Christian Life Today*. New York: Harper & Row, 1965.

Jones, Loyal and Billy Edd Wheeler. *More Laughter in Appalachia*. Atlanta: August House, 2005.

Kohn, Bernice. *The Amistad Mutiny*. New York: McCall, 1971.

Lee, Philip J. *Against the Protestant Gnostics*. New York: Oxford University Press, 1987.

# Bibliography

Lyte, Henry F. "Praise My Soul, the King of Heaven." In *Lutheran Book of Worship*. Minneapolis: Augsburg, 1978.

Macleod, George F. *Only One Way Left: Church Prospect*. Glasgow, UK: The Iona Community, 1964.

Niemöller, Martin. "Current Biography Yearbook." New York: H. W. Wilson, 1965.

Orczy, Emmuska. *The Scarlet Pimpernel*. New York: Bantam Dell, 2007.

Paine, Howard and Bard Thompson. *Book of Prayers for Church and Home*. Philadelphia: The Christian Education, 1962.

Routley, Erik. *Church Music and the Christian Faith*. Carol Stream: Agape, 1978.

Speratus, Paul. "Salvation Unto Us Has Come." In *Evangelical Hymn-Book*. St. Louis: Concordia, 1927.

Sullivan, Herbert and Newman Flower. *Sir Arthur Sullivan: His Life, Letters and Diaries*. New York: George H. Doran, 1927.

Vahanian, Gabriel. *The Death of God*. New York: George Braziller, 1961.

Vitz, Paul. *Psychology as Religion: The Cult of Self-Worship*. Grand Rapids: Eerdmans, 1977.

Yeats, W. B. "Sailing to Byzantium." *Modern Poetry* 7. Ed. Maynard Mack et al. Englewood Cliffs: Prentice Hall, 1961.

Zinn, Howard. *A People's History of the United States, 1492–Present*. New York: Harper Perennial, 1995.

www.ingramcontent.com/pod-product-compliance
Lightning Source LLC
Chambersburg PA
CBHW071504150426
43191CB00009B/1407